M000266556

20 LESSONS
THAT
BUILD A MAN'S
FAITH

A CONVERSATIONAL MENTORING GUIDE

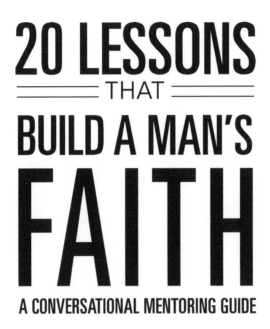

20 LESSONS
== THAT ==
BUILD A MAN'S
FAITH

A CONVERSATIONAL MENTORING GUIDE

VINCE MILLER

EQUIP PRESS

Colorado Springs

WHAT PEOPLE ARE SAYING ABOUT VINCE MILLER

"**V**ince is a man of integrity, a man of character, and of course, a *resolute* man. Through his practical Bible-based writing and speaking he is rapidly becoming one of the most influential leaders of men in the church. When Vince speaks, men listen. Gentlemen, take my advice, read this book, and get building!"

—**Marty Miller,** *President at Blueprint For Men*

"**V**ince Miller's clarion call to men undeniably captures the heart and inspires action. He has a unique ability to challenge and motivate men in positive ways that translate to dynamic results. His commitment to communicating God's truth in a reachable and applicable way makes this resource an invaluable tool in the life of every man."

—**Dave Mergens,** *Men's Pastor*

"**V**ince Miller is a profound leader of men. His ministry has been transformational in my personal growth as a leader. His content is excellent at informing and guiding men to dig deep and face important challenges together, whether it be one-on-one or in a group setting. I am very grateful that through Vince's ministry, I have formed strong relationships that will last a lifetime."

—**Mike Cunningham,** *Men's Leader*

"Vince Miller is a man whose life, speaking, and leadership development ministry is centered on the Gospel of Jesus Christ. The fruit of Vince's life and ministry produces leaders who are personally challenged toward maturity in Christ and are able to train and equip others to spiritual maturity through developing a dependence on God and practical knowledge and application of His Word. Vince's insight into the Bible and how he challenges you to apply the Gospel to how you live and lead will help you build your family on the solid foundation of Jesus Christ."

—**John Dickerman,** *Men's Leader*

"Vince Miller is a game-changer! He has struck the perfect balance of relevant content, timeless wisdom and effective methodology. There's no games or gimmicks, just bold truth, and a compelling invitation to go all in!"

—**Tyler Van Eps,** *Mentor and Men's Leader*

"Vince understands that defining manhood is no simple task and that every culture from the beginning of time has their own set of standards. God's plan "A" for building better men is for men to actively engage in the lives of other men. We see it consistently throughout the Bible. Men learn how to be men from other men – period. I never understood this until I met Vince. It's because of his dedication and passion for building better husbands, fathers, brothers, sons, leaders, and men of God - that I am a better man."

—**Erin Hauber,** *Men's Leader*

"Men's reactions to Vince's message consistently reveal that deep down, most desire to be men of character, but don't always know how or have the courage to do so. Vince's ministry provides potent messages & tools that can and have changed men to carry out lives of leadership with a focus on God. Vince's raw and emotional testimony, along with his deep-rooted desire to mentor, reshapes and restores men spiritually - which in turn benefits countless family members and loved ones."

— **Eric Bryhn,** *Men's Leader*

20 LESSONS
=== THAT ===
BUILD A MAN'S
FAITH

Published by Equip Press, Colorado Springs, CO

Scripture quotations marked (ESV) are taken from The ESV® Bible (The Holy Bible, English Standard Version®) copyright © 2001 by Crossway, a publishing ministry of Good News Publishers. ESV® Text Edition: 2011. The ESV® text has been reproduced in cooperation with and by permission of Good News Publishers.
Unauthorized reproduction of this publication is prohibited. Used by permission.
All rights reserved.

Scripture quotations marked (KJV) are taken from the King James Bible. Accessed on Bible Gateway at www.BibleGateway.com.

Scripture quotations marked (NASB) are taken from the New American Standard Bible® (NASB), copyright © 1960, 1962, 1963, 1968, 1971, 1972, 1973, 1975, 1977, 1995 by The Lockman Foundation, www.Lockman.org. Used by permission.

Scripture quotations marked (NIV) are taken from the Holy Bible, New International Version. Copyright © 1973, 1978, 1984, 2011 by Biblica, Inc.® Used by permission.
All rights reserved worldwide.

Scripture quotations marked (NKJV) are taken from the New King James Version®.
Copyright © 1982 by Thomas Nelson, Inc. Used by permission. All rights reserved.

Scripture quotations marked (NLT) are taken from the Holy Bible, New Living Translation, copyright © 1996, 2004, 2015 by Tyndale House Foundation. Used by permission of Tyndale House Publishers, Inc., Carol Stream, Illinois 60188. All rights reserved.

Scripture quotations marked (NRSV) are taken from the New Revised Standard Version Bible, copyright © 1989 the Division of Christian Education of the National Council of the Churches of Christ in the United States of America. Used by permission. All rights reserved.

First Edition: 2019
20 that Build Men of Faith / Vince Miller
Paperback ISBN: 978-1-946453-95-2
eBook ISBN: 978-1-946453-96-9

EQUIP PRESS
Colorado Springs

TO: _____

FROM: _____

NOTE: _____

_____

_____

_____

_____

_____

_____

_____

_____

_____

_____

_____

_____

_____

_____

CONTENTS

A NOTE FROM THE AUTHOR

I will never forget the moment I made an initial commitment to Jesus Christ. I had discovered a new life, and it was full of emotion and excitement. But the first steps were awkward. More than anything, I wished I'd had two things. First, a simple guide to lead me through the mechanics of things like prayer, Bible reading, devotional times, and the like. And second, another man to show me the way. This book is potentially both of those things—a mentoring guide for those first steps in the faith.

My prayer is that these lessons give you something to discuss with a friend, relative, coworker, or even your spouse and children. I hope they will stir a discussion that will give you an opportunity to proactively pass on wisdom. May this mentoring relationship lead to greater success as you lead your business, team, non-profit, church, or your very own family.

Join in a mentorship movement, and mentor or be mentored.

Live all in,

USING 20 LESSONS THAT BUILD A MAN'S FAITH

The Purpose

This 20-lesson guide is for mentors to use in private reflection or conversations with others. It's written to invite faith development conversations for men of any age and can be used repeatedly.

The Process

First, build yourself

Read through one lesson each time and ponder privately on the reflection questions within the lesson. Each lesson uses the B.U.I.L.D. process.

- BEGIN with the goal.
- UNPACK your thoughts.
- INFORM through the Bible.
- LAND on action steps.
- DO one action for one week.

Second, partner up

Take each lesson further by partnering up with someone else. Use the 20 lessons as a mentoring tool that takes all the guesswork out of a faith development conversation. Partner up with a brother, relative, co-worker, or someone in your family.

The Payoff

If you stay with the process for all 20 lessons, you will grow in character, in your leadership, and in community with others. Often, we just need a plan to get moving. This book provides that plan—a method and a process that results in outcomes with a rich payoff.

SPEAKER & AUTHOR VINCE MILLER

Abandoned by his drug-using father at the age of two, Vince Miller grew up in a challenging and anxiety-producing environment. He endured the strain of his mother's two failed marriages as well as her poor choices and drug use. Fortunately, during Vince's formative teen years, his grandfather, a man of faith, stepped up to mentor Vince, guiding him through a particularly difficult period.

Though he resisted initially, Vince became a follower of Christ at the age of 20. Soon after, he would be with his grandfather on his deathbed as cancer took his life. At that time, Vince committed before God to give back by mentoring men as his grandfather had mentored him. Vince's story demonstrates the importance of mentors to support others in overcoming the enormous hurdles that manhood, mentoring, fathering, and leadership present to a man who wants to live in faith and character.

Audiences respond to Vince's stories and teaching that motivate, convict, and sometimes even shock. He inspires men to lead and mentor others with an intelligent argument for faith and stories of choices he made as a man, husband, father, and leader.

After serving in notable organizations for over 26 years (including Young Life, InterVarsity, and TCU Football), Vince founded Resolute, a non-profit organization focused on providing men with tools for mentorship. He's written 16 books and Bible study handbooks, along with small group videos that are resources for mentorship. He also produces a daily writing known as The Men's Daily Devotional, read by thousands daily.

If you are looking for a motivational and engaging communicator for your next retreat, conference, or event, reach out to Vince Miller directly through his website at www.vincemiller.com.

Scripture: The Importance

"The Bible is the book of my life. It's the book I live with, the book I live by, the book I want to die by."

—N. T. WRIGHT

All Scripture is breathed out by God and profitable for teaching, for reproof, for correction, and for training in righteousness, that the man of God may be complete, equipped for every good work"

—2 TIMOTHY 3:14-17

Why Study the Scripture?

You know the drill! You've probably been told that you need to study Scripture regularly, but why? Isn't attending church and occasionally visiting a small group enough—so why is it so important to read and study the Bible yourself? It's a great and vital question. And many of the answers are found in these words of the Apostle Paul in the book of Romans.

"I appeal to you therefore, brothers, by the mercies of God,
to present your bodies as a living sacrifice, holy and acceptable to
God, which is your spiritual worship. Do not be conformed to
this world, but be transformed by the renewal of your mind, that by

testing you may discern what is the will of God, what is good
and acceptable and perfect."

—Romans 12:1-2

Three Reasons to Study Scripture

One | It's our guide to transformation

When Paul tells you not to conform any longer to the pattern of this world, he is reminding you that the design of the world, or the way the world thinks, is different from how God thinks. In almost every field of life: marriage, sexuality, ethics, finances, priorities, etc., God's teaching is in opposition to what the world considers truth. Paul suggests the solution to this conflict is subjecting your mind to renewal by testing the opinions of the world against God's truth. And this is where Scripture comes in.

In a letter to his protégé, Timothy, Paul reminds him of the importance of Scripture in his life.

> *"But as for you, continue in what you have learned and have*
> *firmly believed, knowing from whom you learned it and how from*
> *childhood you have been acquainted with the sacred writings, which*
> *are able to make you wise for salvation through faith in Christ Jesus.*
> *All Scripture is breathed out by God and profitable for teaching, for*
> *reproof, for correction, and for training in righteousness, that the*
> *man of God may be complete, equipped for every good work"*

—2 Timothy 3:14-17.

It's the Scriptures that plum your thinking against truth and renews your mind. It's God's way of constantly reminding you of His perspective on truth, life, and godliness. God's Word shows you the path, when you get off the path, how to get back on the path, and how to stay on the path.

And every time you discover new truths from God's Word and apply them, you discover freedom because living a life of truth keeps you from the traps along the path of life. With this perspective, you find out Scripture requires a daily process that guides you to your freedom in Christ. And who doesn't want that? Like breathing induces oxygen to our lungs, Scripture induces truth to our lives. It's God's breath, or oxygen, that encourages, corrects, trains, teaches, and convicts so that we are equipped *"for every good work."*

Two | It works in partnership with the Holy Spirit

As Christ followers, we are empowered by something others do not possess—the Holy Spirit. As the third person of the Godhead, He is our counselor who guides us into all truth because He is the *"Spirit of truth"—John 14:17*. When you combine the truth of God's Word with the Spirit of Truth who convicts you according to God's Word and guides you to apply it, you have a powerful God-given combination that ushers in change.

This dynamic is addressed in Hebrews 4:12-13. *"For the word of God is living and active, sharper than any two-edged sword, piercing to the division of soul and of spirit, of joints and of marrow, and discerning the thoughts and intentions of the heart. And no creature is hidden from his sight, but all are naked and exposed to the eyes of him to whom we must give account."* Scriptures are living and active because God breath and the Holy Spirit within you is present as you read, reflect, and study them. And it's this Spirit that reinforces the truth of Scripture to penetrate your desires, thoughts, and behaviors.

Three | It's one way we encounter God

Time spent in God's Word is not the same as in other books you might read or study. When you read Scripture, you get the pleasure of encountering God. And as you meet God, you are changed by an unchanging God who possesses timeless truth. And in the process, you become more like Him. This is a living, dynamic encounter with God. The more time you spend with Him, the more opportunities you have to renew your mind and become like Him in how you think, feel, and behave.

How many times have you wished that you could sit down with Jesus face to face and ask Him questions? Gain his wisdom? Ask his advice? Or receive his encouragement? Every time you open Scripture, that's what is happening. Truth is there. Encouragement is there. Wisdom is there. And, God is there. Don't miss out on what could be the best part of your day and life. Start with even a little bit of Scripture every day.

Reflection & Mentorship

Begin

- Scripture is our path to whole-life transformation in partnership with the Spirit and one way we build a growing relationship with God.

Unpack

- What factors make reading Scripture intimidating?
- What is one story you have either read or heard told from the Bible, and what corresponding lesson have you learned?

Inform

- Hebrews states that the Bible is *"living and active."* What do you think the writer meant by this statement?
- Which of the three points in the lesson above stood out to you?

Land

- List 1-3 personal challenges you encounter as you read the Scripture. Be honest.
- What corresponding steps do you need to take to overcome these personal challenges?

Do

- This week either: choose a verse from the Bible and act on it or choose a personal challenge with Scripture and take one action to overcome it. Either way, do something.
- When you do take one of the actions above, share the result with a friend or mentor.

Scripture: Memorizing It

> "The Bible in the memory is better
> than the Bible in the bookcase."

—CHARLES HADDON SPURGEON

> "I have stored up your word in my heart,
> that I might not sin against you."

—PSALM 119:11

I Want to Memorize Scripture but I'm Not Sure I Can

If you are anything like me, you struggle to memorize anything. However, over the years, I have gotten exceedingly better at memorizing Scripture— even entire chapters of the text. And for most, Scripture memorization feels like a daunting task. And the older you get, the less you feel confident you can pull it off. It's a discipline most desire but don't know how to tackle.

Four Steps to Memorizing Scripture

One | Learn the context

The first tip is to study the verse or verses you want to memorize in their context. The context helps you understand the fuller concept of the verse.

Verses don't stand alone—with the exception of perhaps a few of the Proverbs. Every verse has a context. The context provides you an understanding of the characters and the setting and gives you a visual image to memorize along with the words—which aids retention.

For instance, John 3:16—unquestionably the most famous verse in the Bible—is not a stand-alone verse. It's a moment of tension in a critical story where Jesus is discussing eternal life as he engages with a religious man named Nicodemus. Knowing this not only helps you understand John 3:16, but it also enables you to remember that this verse contains key principles on new life in Christ with a person who was religious but struggled to understand the more in-depth teaching of Jesus. While you may memorize the text, you also now have a context for the story. The context reinforces the memory of the words. They are both words and a story that is full of emotion, tension, and truth.

Two | Break verses into phrases

When you start memorizing the verse, taking into consideration its context, the next step is to break the verse down into bite-size phrases. Memorization includes savoring the phrases, understanding them, internalizing them, and meditating on them. Think about these phrases that make up John 3:16.

For God so loved the world,
that he gave his only Son,
that whoever believes in him
should not perish
but have eternal life.

Rather than mindlessly trying to memorize the verse, it is far better to meditate on each of the phrases that make up the verse, thinking of their meaning. In this way internalize the verse until it is not only memorized, but it's meaning instilled in your mind. Using this methodology, you can remember any verse without focusing on the memorization but the meaning. The memorization becomes a byproduct of your meditating.

Three | Use the verses

One of the keys to retention is to use what you have memorized as often as possible until it becomes fixed in your thinking, action, and behavior. Practice, for instance, using the verse or verses memorized in prayer. Write them in your journal. If you have an accountability partner or mentor, share them. Repeat them silently to yourself. Use them as passwords, for example, "FGsltwthghoStwbihsnpbhel-J316" is a pretty secure password, and it's easy for you to remember—eventually. Everyone learns differently, so try using various tactics as you memorize the text. As you do, recall the context in which the verse(s) is found and remind yourself of the larger picture.

Meditation is a crucial outcome of using the verses as mentioned above. Meditation infers we are thinking about it and the various ways it applies to our everyday life. Remember that your goal is not how many verses one can memorize but how well you can use the verse to your life. Memorizing verses and reflecting on their application to your life is a key both to remembering and to applying. The more you think about what you have implanted through memorization, the more insights you will have for your own life, which leads right into the last principle.

Four | Be changed

We are called to use Scripture to renew the mind. And there is no better way to renew our minds than by saturating it with God's Word. Our brains are wired to assimilate vast amounts of information, and those pieces of information create neuron pathways for good or for evil that are not easy to change. If we fill our minds with lies, our brains develop paths that desire more distortion. If we fill our minds with God's Word, our brains create essential pathways that are life-giving rather than life-stealing.

David writes in Psalm 119:36, *"Incline my heart to your testimonies, and not to selfish gain!"* There are many trivial things we can load into our mind. God's Word implanted there renews our lives, actions, and behaviors. So, don't only memorize the words, apply them. Live them. In the case of John 3:16, you might choose today to believe in Him when it seems unreasonable, challenging, or even uncomfortable—like it was for Nicodemus. Maybe you need to take your belief to the next level? Apply it. Live it. Try it and be changed.

Reflection & Mentorship

Begin

- Memorizing Scripture is easier when you learn the context, break verse into phrases, use the verses, and let the words change you.

Unpack

- Is Scripture memorization easy or hard for you? Or have you even tried to memorize Scripture before?
- What types of memorization are easier for you—memorizing images, concepts, processes, or words? Why do you think this is?
- How could you use a memorization approach that is easier for you and apply it to Scripture memorization?

Inform

- Psalm 119:11 says, *"I have stored up your word in my heart, that I might not sin against you."* How does memorizing Scripture help us based on this one verse?
- If you memorized 52 verses this year, that's one a week, how

would that impact your view and relationship with God based on Psalm 119:11?

Land

- What issues need to be addressed for you memorize 10-20 Scriptures this year?
- What steps need to be taken to address the issue or issues you just mentioned?

Do

- What one Scripture will you memorize this week? If you don't know, be committed to finding one that applies to your life and communicate it back to a friend or mentor.
- Spend one week using the four steps above for Scripture memorization.
- Share the verse in a number of ways with people you encounter this week and, if possible, with your friend or mentor.

Scripture: Meditating on It

"Worry is focused thinking on something negative.
Meditation is doing the same thing only focusing on God's
Word instead of your problem."

—RICK WARREN

"I will meditate on your precepts and fix my eyes
on your ways."

—PSALM 119:15

Four questions about meditation and the steps to help you start.

The Scriptures talk a great deal about meditation, especially in the books of wisdom like Psalms, Proverbs, Ecclesiastes, and Job. But what does meditation mean, what happens when I do it, what are the benefits, and how do I do it? Here is one definition:

*"Meditation in the Bible means reflective thinking on biblical,
truth so that God can speak to us through Scripture and through the
thoughts that come to mind as we are reflecting on the Word, but that
must also be filtered by the Word."*

—bible.org

29

What Is Meditation?

In other words, meditation is the practice of taking a verse or many verses and then contemplating, deliberating, and mulling over those verses and their implications for our lives in the course of a few minutes, a day, or longer. As we consider the biblical truth, God's voice has the opportunity to enlighten us on how that truth applies to our lives.

What Happens When We Meditate?

Meditation has the potential to bring ongoing transformation to our lives over time. Paul exhorts us in Romans 12:2, *"Do not conform any longer to the pattern of this world but be transformed by the renewing of your mind. Then you will be able to test and approve what God's will is—His good, pleasing and perfect will."* As we meditate on specific passages in God's Word, the truths of that passage become resident in our minds and once *in residence,* they influence our thinking and our actions.

Consider, for instance, Micah 6:8. *"He has told you, O man, what is good; and what does the Lord require of you but to do justice, and to love kindness, and to walk humbly with your God?"* Think of all the biblical truths packed into that one verse and the many implications it has for our lives. I would encourage you to meditate on that one verse this coming week as a test drive for how God's Word can become resident in your life. Meditate on it, pray on it, and act on it as situations present themselves.

What Are the Benefits of Meditation?

Scripture mentions many ways that meditation helps us live out our Christian lives in ways that please God:

- It focuses our minds (Ps 119:15).
- It helps us better understand (Ps 119:27).
- It helps us remember God's faithfulness to us (Ps 143:5).

- It facilitates worship (Ps 1:2).
- It helps us apply God's Word (Titus 3:3-4).

All of these allow the Word of God to take up residence in our hearts and lives, adjust our mindset to God's thinking, and help us live out the truths on a daily basis.

How Do I Start?

A simple way to facilitate meditation is to take the verse, or verses, from the Men's Daily Devotional (www.beresolute.org/mdd) for the day and print them out for the car, your desk at work, and wherever you spend your time. Ask Jesus to transform your mind, thinking and life as you meditate on his eternal word.

Reflection & Mentorship

Begin

- Meditation is a purposeful reflection on Biblical truths so that God can convict and change us.

Unpack

- The word *"meditation"* has a mystic feeling and meaning to people today. Why do we hold this view of meditation?
- Practically, we are always meditating on something. What do most men spend most of their time meditating on?

Inform

- Romans 12:1-2 reads, *"Do not conform any longer to the pattern of this world but be transformed by the renewing of your mind. Then*

you will be able to test and approve what God's will is—His good, pleasing and perfect will." What does this say about the danger of meditating on the wrong thing?
- But what is the impact of meditating on the right thing?

Land

- What obvious issues do you face in taking time to meditate?
- What steps do you need to take to overcome these issues?
- How could you build meditation into your everyday life?

Do

- What is one thing you want to stop meditating on this week?
- What one thing do you want to start meditating on from God's truth?
- Act on the two items you just discussed and follow up with a friend or mentor within the next week.

The Discipline of Time with God

"Spending time with God is the key to our strength and success in all areas of life. Be sure that you never try to work God into your schedule, but always work your schedule around Him."

—JOYCE MEYER

"I am the vine; you are the branches. Whoever abides in me and I in him, he it is that bears much fruit, for apart from me you can do nothing. If anyone does not abide in me he is thrown away like a branch and withers; and the branches are gathered, thrown into the fire, and burned. If you abide in me, and my words abide in you, ask whatever you wish, and it will be done for you. By this my Father is glorified, that you bear much fruit and so prove to be my disciples."

—JOHN 15:5-8

A necessary appointment

Our lives are filled with appointments and meetings, but there is one appointment that we find hard to keep consistent. And missing this one appointment produces guilt and failure in many men—it's having a regular time with God. But this regular appointment with God doesn't have to be so daunting. It should be a source of life, joy, truth, direction, and a means of deepening our relationship with the God who loves us.

Things to remember and do

One | Remember God loves our company

It's hard to comprehend but God created us for a relationship with him, and he loves when we choose to spend time with him. Often, I picture God sitting in an empty chair across from me when I take time to be with him. After all, he's there with me. I imagine myself talking to a close friend who happens to be the Creator of the universe. Men like Moses, Abraham, David, Joshua, and even Jesus inferred that they communicated with God in much the same way. Often, they prayed out loud just like they would any other conversation. These conversations were how they invested in what was a primary and essential relationship for them.

We wouldn't dream of neglecting a close friend, our spouse, or a child. We spend time with these people because they give us life, connection, wisdom, and support. We need their companionship in regular doses. And it's no different with God, except he's not just any friend or relationship, he's the ultimate source of life. Jesus put it this way:

> *"I am the vine; you are the branches. Whoever abides in me and I in him, he it is that bears much fruit, for apart from me you can do nothing. If anyone does not abide in me he is thrown away like a branch and withers; and the branches are gathered, thrown into the fire, and burned. If you abide in me, and my words abide in you, ask whatever you wish, and it will be done for you. By this my Father is glorified, that you bear much fruit and so prove to be my disciples."*
>
> –John 15:5-8.

Did you notice the operative word in Jesus' instruction? It's remaining–remaining in him. And having a daily quiet time with God is a vital method for *"remaining in him and he in us."*

Two | Don't overcomplicate it

What kinds of things do you do in a relationship with someone you love or care about? You invest time with them. At times, it's as simple as a quick phone call, to hear what's going on with them and sharing what's going on with you. It is no different when we meet with God. We take some time alone with God, maybe 6-12 minutes at the start of each day. During this time, listen to him by reading a text from his Word, and talk to him in conversational prayer. Sometimes you might like to prepare yourself with a song of worship at the start as a way of praising him.

Think of your meeting with God as an alignment meeting to get each day started right. In quietness, bring your needs to him, confess your sin, ask for his help, learn from him through meditation on the text, and worship him as Lord. Time with him daily will incrementally change your heart and mind, and as a result, you will become more like him.

Three | Remember to keep it regular

Our relationship with God is only as new as the last time we were with him. So keep it regular with a daily appointment. Sometimes it may be just touching base for a few minutes. And other times we may have more extended time with him, but don't neglect the best and most forgiving, loving, and gracious friend you will ever have—God.

A Suggested Pattern

[2-3 Minutes] Preparing for the meeting

Start to slow by preparing for your quiet time with a period of silence, praise, or reflection. The goal in preparation is to move from thinking about the cares of the world to thinking about your relationship with God.

During this time, you will want to note where you are at personally and the current state of your heart, mind, and soul. It may be good to write out critical concerns in a journal or notepad so that you can move from your self-concerns to a posture of engaging God.

[2-3 Minutes] Listen to God by reading a relevant Scripture

Next, take a couple of minutes to find verses that speak to the concerns you noted. I love the Open Bible's Topic search tool for this: www.openbible. info/topics. Just type in a word or phrase and you will find a ton of relevant verses. Stop at the one that speaks to you and listen to God's Word to you. During this time just let God speak. Read the verse multiple times looking at God's instruction for your situation. It might be good to write out the action or steps God's Word suggests you take.

[2-3 Minutes] Talk to God by sharing your needs

Finally, talk to God about your situation, the direction Scripture is leading you, and the challenges you are facing. The A.C.T.S. method is a great model for this conversation time. It begins with **Adoration**—revering God for what he has done. Next, **Confess**—this is to own the sin that God has brought to your mind during your reading. Next, **Thanksgiving**—appreciate God for what he has done or revealed to you. Finally, **Supplication**—ask God for what you might need for the day. We will discuss this method in more detail in a coming chapter.

In 6-12 daily minutes, you will not only be centered for a new day, but you will deepen your relationship with the God of the universe who wants to be in a loving relationship with you. Try this pattern for 30 days and your relationship with God will be more profound and the outcomes unbelievable.

Reflection & Mentorship

Begin

- Regular time with God is as important, if not more important than, as relationships with other people, we have to choose to invest in it.

Unpack

- Spending time with God on a regular basis sounds odd for men in a new relationship with him. What makes this new behavior odd and different from other relationships?
- What have you heard that most Christian men do in a regular time with God?

Inform

- John 15:5 reads, *"Whoever abides in me and I in him, he it is that bears much fruit, for apart from me you can do nothing."* What does the word abide mean?
- What activities are involved in abiding?
- What are the outputs of abiding?
- What are the outputs of not abiding?

Land

- Do you have a regular time with God each day?
- What would you like to see happen in your regular time with God?

Do

- Set a regular time with God each day this week. Determine a meeting time and location.

- Try the suggested pattern above in each of these scheduled meetings.
- Discuss the experience and outputs of this experience in one week with a friend or mentor and tweak it if needed to your liking.

The Discipline of Journaling

"I want to write, but more than that, I want to bring out all kinds of things that lie buried deep in my heart."

—ANNE FRANK

"My God, my God, why have you forsaken me?"

—PSALM 21:1,
(written in David's journal and repeated by Jesus on the cross.)

Journaling is an ancient discipline

Journaling is one of the oldest of the spiritual disciplines. It is the reason we have such wonderful spiritual insights from so many men of faith who have gone before us and who have influenced God's people for hundreds of years. In many ways, the Psalms were mostly the private journal entries of King David as he meditated and reflected on God and the Scriptures. And the Proverbs were the individual journal reflections of King Solomon, to pass on the wisdom we need for greater success.

All men should try journaling if you currently do not. The practice can be life-changing. Here are three reasons why you should.

Three Reasons You Should Journal

One | Journaling helps your mind to focus

Most of us have many streams of thought, concerns, and challenges running through our minds at any one time. This is normal, as our minds are often processing multiple issues in the backdrop. And this is fine, except that there are many times when it is essential to focus on specific topics so that we can come to clarity on those issues, as every part of life is part of our followership of Jesus. Journaling helps the mind to focus sharply on matters that might need prayer and attention in our lives and let go of the peripheral issue that might be keeping us from disciplining the mind.

Two | Journaling helps you to process

Suppose we are having trouble relating to one of our children or are in a struggle with them about specific behaviors. We are frustrated and irritated and cannot figure out how to approach them or deal with their actions. There is nothing like a journal to help us think through our approaches, responses, the issues at stake, and which hills to die on and which to let go. Journaling helps us focus on an issue, so we think it through, and it helps us process our thinking, behaviors, reactions, or actions.

Think again of the Psalms or what I refer to as King David's private journal. Psalm 23 was an entry that helped him process and put into perspective the presence of God in good times and bad. And then Psalm 51 helped him reflect on his sin and God's incredible forgiveness. Every time we journal, we are clarifying and processing, which is the genius of the activity.

Three | Journaling records your growth

Few things are more gratifying than to look back over time and see our growth. When we have a written record, we can go back and see what issue was troubling us a year ago is now resolved because we have grown wiser. We can look at the challenges we survived, marriages that have gotten stronger, relationships which are being healed and through all of these we see how Jesus has been faithful to us. We can also see more readily with hindsight the work of the Holy Spirit in our lives. Our journals are a record of our growth, which accelerates as we journal because we have learned to focus on critical issues in our lives and process through them.

Reflection & Mentorship

Begin

- Journaling is an ancient activity with numerous benefits. It helps us focus, process, and record our growth.

Unpack

- Have you ever tried journaling? What were the pros and cons of the experience?
- When you work, do you ever take notes? What are the benefits and reasons for doing this?

Inform

- In Psalm 21:1, David wrote, *"My God, my God, why have you forsaken me?"* How do you think David was feeling when he wrote this?
- Have you felt like this before?
- Why did Jesus repeat these words on the cross during his crucifixion?
- Do you think Jesus would have said it if David had not written it down?
- What does this infer about the importance of journaling?

Land

- What issues prevent you from the practice of journaling?
- What steps do you need to take to address these obstacles?

Do

- Try journaling three times this week.
- Share some or part of journal entries with a friend or mentor.

The Bible: The Structure

> "Most people are bothered by those passages of Scripture
> they do not understand, but the passages that bother me are
> those I do understand."
>
> **—MARK TWAIN**

> "You shall teach them to your children, talking of them when
> you are sitting in your house, and when you are walking by
> the way, and when you lie down, and when you rise."
>
> **—DEUTERONOMY 11:19**

It's intimidating

Are you intimidated by the Bible, with its couple of thousand text-dense pages? If so, you're not alone. Too many Bibles sit on end tables and nightstands, bindings uncracked. Why is it so hard to get into God's Word?

We've already touched on part of the answer—the Bible is a big book! But many of us also struggle with a fear of the unknown. We may have grown up hearing lots of Bible stories, but we don't know too much about the book itself. So let's learn a few Bible basics—let's demystify the Scriptures with a brief overview so that we can start enjoying the riches it contains.

The Key Parts

Part One | The Old Testament

Maybe it'll help to think of the Bible not as one big book, but rather as a collection of books gathered in one volume. The first 39 books make up what we call the Old Testament—all the stuff that happened before Jesus came along. Talk about adventure and suspense, comedy and drama, history and romance, mystery and intrigue, heroes and villains—the Bible has it all. We find ourselves engrossed in the story of creation, the patriarchs of the faith, the Exodus from Egypt, the conquest of Israel, the time of the judges, the succession of kings, the war within Israel, and the period of rebuilding. And threaded through it all is a three-faceted theme: the problem of evil, the redemption of man, and the need for faith in God.

Part Two | The New Testament

The New Testament comprises 27 books and personal letters that relate the good news of God's grace and mercy, and the salvation He makes possible through His Son Jesus Christ. The first four books—the Gospels of Matthew, Mark, Luke, and John—chronicle Jesus' birth, life, ministry, death, and resurrection, setting the stage for the building of His church. What follows are the often heart-wrenching writings of His disciples as they established the church, corresponded with local bodies of believers and their leaders, and carried Jesus' message to the rest of the known world.

Part Three | The "Meta-Narrative"

The meta-narrative, the focus of the entire Bible, is, of course, Jesus Christ Himself. He is what ties it all together—every theme, story, and promise from the Old Testament points to Him and is fulfilled in Him. We discover in the New Testament that Jesus becomes the new:

- ADAM—perfect as a man.
- KING—appointed by God.
- KINGDOM—establishing one out of all nations.
- TEMPLE—constructed in the heart of a man by the Holy Spirit.
- PRIEST—who offers a propitiation for sins.
- ATONEMENT—who atones for all sin at all time.
- SACRIFICE—giving his life on the cross for us.
- JUDGE—who is just in all dealings.
- CREATION—dying to create a new life.
- LAW—one governed by grace through faith.

We call the Bible *God's Word* because He inspired it. He reveals Himself in its pages, and to read it, ponder it, study it, and even commit it to memory is to know Him better and better. So, let's stop cheating ourselves of the wisdom, instruction, inspiration, and joy to be found between its opening words *"In the beginning..."* and its final *"Amen"*—and get up close and personal with our Father, the Creator and King of the universe.

Reflection & Mentorship

Begin

- The Bible is a book full of stories that tell one major story about God and his interaction with the world through Jesus and the expansion of his message throughout the world.

Unpack

- What is one Bible story you recall from the Bible?
- What is the meaning of this story?
- How does this story connect to the meta-narrative of the Bible?

Inform

- Deuteronomy 11:19 reads, *"You shall teach them to your children, talking of them when you are sitting in your house, and when you are walking by the way, and when you lie down, and when you rise."* Engagement with the Bible was a requirement of spiritual leaders in the family. How is this charge challenging for leaders in the home today?
- What activities are involved in *"teaching to your children"* in the text?

Land

- What challenges do you encounter when reading the text of the Bible?
- How could reading the Bible more, or just spending more time in the Bible, help you with these challenges?

Do

- Read one short book of the New Testament this week like Galatians, Ephesians, Philippians, Colossians, Philemon, Titus, 1, 2, or 3 John, or Jude.
- Try remembering the themes and applications.
- Apply the lesson you have learned and share it with a friend or mentor.

The Bible: Read It

I want to know one thing, the way to heaven: how to land
safe on that happy shore. God himself has condescended to
teach the way; for this very end he came from heaven. He has
written it down in a book! Oh, give me that book! At any price,
give me the book of God! I have it: here is knowledge enough
for me. Let me be: "A man of one book."

—JOHN WESLEY

"Your word is a lamp to my feet and a light to my path."

—PSALM 119:105

We Are Buying Them, But We Aren't Reading Them

Many who are followers of Christ today confess that they are not familiar with Scripture. The statistics on this are actually alarming. Many Christians, regardless of their spiritual age, tend to leave matters of observation, interpretation, and application of the Scripture up to their pastors, trained professionals, supplemental books, or sermons rather than digging into the Bible on their own. But the Bible, unsurpassed as the best-selling book of all time, was meant to be read, studied, and understood by the general population, not exclusively church leaders. We're all called to be students of the Scriptures. Yet for many, it's not a lack of interest, but rather the intimidation factor, as it's unlike any other book a person will ever read. It was written by 40 authors, over two thousand years, to people in times in which we did not live. It's not a common reader like the business, self-help, or fiction books you find on the shelf today. Yet God wants you to uncover its mysteries and truth. And here's how.

Just Read It

Yes, I am suggesting that you read the whole Bible, the whole way through, as painful as it might be. A surprising number of Christians never regularly read parts of the Bible, much less the whole thing. Yet it's the central message of their faith. If that is you, then find a One-Year Bible Reading Plan and read through the Bible so that you have some frame of reference for the entire book. The best way to do this is to partner with a man or a few other men and read it over one year together. Yes, a year is a long time, but with other men, it becomes a lot more interesting, inviting, and invigorating. It's like working out together, you may read some on your own, but with accountability from other men, you might hang in there all the way through one entire year. Along the way, you will have the opportunity to discuss what you are reading and encourage each other in the journey. Together, you will experience a sense of accomplishment, accountability, and an appreciation for Scripture that only comes from diving in. Some men I know repeat this annually, using a different version of the Bible for a change of pace that keeps it fresh.

After you do this, or maybe while you are doing this, you can dive in a little deeper. And here is how.

First | Read an entire book in the Bible

Here's what I mean. The Bible is one book containing 66 books; 39 are Old Testament books and 27 are New Testament books. They are independent writings written for specific people at specific times. Choose one to read in its entirety. For instance, to study through the Gospel of John, start by reading the whole Gospel once or twice to get an overview of the book. Getting a picture of the whole is just as important as taking portions for further study. This gives you a strong context for the characters, storyline, genres, styles, tone, and themes of the book. While you could consult a commentary on this subject, you don't need it in most cases. Simply take notes, write down what you learn, ask questions, follow the people and the tension, and take in the fuller context. Most fail to do this and, therefore, make a critical error in understanding the meaning the writer intended; thus, they make wrong personal application to their life. But you must have a context before you start interpreting and applying the lessons of the text; otherwise, you will end up drawing misaligned conclusions.

Second | Focus on drawing meaning from a section

Take a section, as your Bible outlines it, for one study, and dig into what the author wanted the original audience to know. Notice what was said there. Remember, your Bible was not written to you; it was written to the people in that day and time. Because of this, they would have heard and understood things differently than you would today. Their culture, customs, and practices were very different from ours; therefore, each text has an intended meaning to them. And this is what we want to discover.

Most Bibles have section headings, often two to three per chapter, which delineates paragraphs that fit together into a specific topic. In daily Scripture study, it is valuable to work through a specific book of Scripture a section at a time. Read each section thoroughly and ask yourself—*"What did the author want the people of their day to understand through this teaching?"*

To put it another way, there is a reason that God included what is written in our Bibles. If you can ascertain what the writer wanted us to know, you will be better able to answer the next question.

Third | Discover the application

Here is where the Scriptures get personal. Paul tells Timothy that *"all Scripture is breathed out by God and profitable for teaching, for reproof, for correction, and for training in righteousness"—2 Timothy 3:16*. So ask yourself these questions:

- Is the text teaching me in some way?
- Is the text rebuking me in some way?
- Is the text correcting me in some way?
- Is the text training me in some way?

This is where a journal becomes very useful. Jot down any observations you made as you considered what the author intended to convey and then specific applications for your life. Speaking of jotting things down, make the Bible yours by marking it up, making notes, and underlining portions that are especially meaningful to you. There are pens made for writing in the margins or underlining that don't bleed through. You will remember what you have studied much better if you make notes as you go, whether in your journal or in your Bible. Or maybe try both.

You will encounter hard sayings or passages difficult to understand, and, in those cases, you may want to purchase a commentary—many are very easy to read and not technical. Be careful, however, to first do your own study and make your own observations before reading a commentary. The longer you study the Bible, the more you will understand, and you will start to see themes that run through the Bible.

Four | Ask for insight

Because the Holy Spirit leads us into all truth (see John 14), specifically ask the Holy Spirit to reveal to you what He wants you to understand and apply. Scripture study for the building knowledge that excludes spiritual transformation is a missed opportunity. Knowledge is good for awareness and personal pride, but devoid of personal and spiritual transformation, it leaves us wanting more. God gave us the Word for transformation, which moves us toward reconciliation and redemption in our world.

If you need help in studying the Bible on a regular basis, find another guy who does it regularly and asks him to mentor you for a time. Study some passages together so that you start to feel comfortable doing it yourself. At the end of your life, you will never regret the time and effort you put into studying God's Word, or the difference it made in your life.

Reflection & Mentorship

Begin

- Having a Bible is important but reading it regularly is where we find value for life and godliness.

Unpack

- How many Bibles do you think most families own?
- How often do you think these Christian families read them?
- How many Bibles do you have?
- How often do you really read them? (Be honest with yourself)

Inform

- Psalm 119:105 reads, *"Your word is a lamp to my feet and a light to my path."*
- What does the phrase *"lamp to my feet"* infer about the Bible and God's Word?
- What does the phrase *"light to my path"* infer about the Bible and God's Word?

Land

- What issues do you need to address in gleaning application from the Bible?
- What do you need to do to more quickly apply what you learn from the Bible?

Do

- Find a verse from the New Testament that you need to apply this week to a challenge you are facing.
- Memorize this verse, and text it to 1-5 people.
- Apply it and share the results in one week with a friend or mentor.

The Bible: How to Study It

"Reading gives us breadth, but study gives us depth."

—JERRY BRIDGES

"Do your best to present yourself to God as one approved, a worker who has no need to be ashamed, rightly handling the word of truth."

—2 TIMOTHY 2:15

An Age-Old Method That Will Make You Look as Smart as Your Pastor

Let's face it. Many of us find the idea of personal Bible study daunting, especially if we haven't done it before. Don't you have to be a trained theologian to study Scripture effectively? Nope! While there are truths that we will never fully grasp because God is so amazingly great, His Word is understandable for all of us, especially if we take the time to study it on a regular basis. So what is the secret to studying the Bible on our own?

Three Simple Steps to Bible Study

One | Observation – What does the passage say?

This step may seem straightforward, but that isn't always true. Many of us bring our own theological biases to our reading of Scripture because we have been told what our theological perspective ought to be. All of our perspectives are deficient in some way, so it's essential to allow the text to speak for itself. Just ask the question, *"What does it say?"*

Two | Interpretation – What does the passage mean?

This step involves discerning the author's main thought or idea behind what he is writing. So you want to pay attention to the five C's here: What was the **context** of the passage; are there **cross-references** where the Bible talks about the same issue (Scripture interprets Scripture); what was the **cultural** context in that day; what is your **conclusion** as to what the passage means and if necessary consult a **commentary** where you have additional questions. While that may sound complicated, it isn't, and most of the time the meaning will be evident quickly.

Three | Application – What am I going to do about what the passage means and says?

This step is where first-time readers begin rather than end. They love to know the truths of Scripture, but they don't relish applying those truths that are inconvenient. But Scripture study without personal application is a waste of time and does not honor God. The good news is that God always blesses any effort we make to bring our lives into conformity with His Word. And His Holy Spirit will help us make that a reality if we are committed to the simple principle of taking God at His word and following His commands and teaching.

There are few more exciting things than to discover God, understand His plan for our lives, and see His character become our character. The book of Proverbs describes the process as being like a miner who searches for silver and gold and finds it after hard work. Every nugget in their search is a reward, and every nugget of truth discovered in Scripture is our reward as it is applied and lived out.

As you engage in your mining of God's Word, keep a journal and jot down your discoveries. Then pray over those discoveries that God would help you apply the truths you found to your life.

Reflection & Mentorship

Begin

- Bible study method that is inductive, draws meaning from the text, and helps us draw the right conclusions.

Unpack

- Deductive reading is different from inductive reading. Deductive reading draws conclusions first before studying. Inductive reading draws meaning from a more careful reading. So how do you think most people read the Bible?
- Have you ever studied Scripture using the Inductive process above? What benefits does this have for the reader?

Inform

- Read the following text and then follow the inductive process above.
- *"Blessed be the God and Father of our Lord Jesus Christ, who has blessed us in Christ with every spiritual blessing in the heavenly places, even as he chose us in him before the foundation of the world, that*

we should be holy and blameless before him. In love he predestined us for adoption to himself as sons through Jesus Christ, according to the purpose of his will, to the praise of his glorious grace, with which he has blessed us in the Beloved. In him we have redemption through his blood, the forgiveness of our trespasses, according to the riches of his grace, which he lavished upon us, in all wisdom and insight making known to us the mystery of his will, according to his purpose, which he set forth in Christ as a plan for the fullness of time, to unite all things in him, things in heaven and things on earth." —Ephesians 1:3-10*

- What observations and interpretations did you make?

Land

- What application did you make from the text?
- What steps do you need to take to live differently?

Do

- Choose one chapter from a book of the Bible to study inductively for the next week.
- Draw application from it for the next week.
- Report back to a friend or mentor what you have learned from reading the Bible this way.

Prayer: The Outcomes

"The purpose of prayer is emphatically not to bend God's will to ours, but rather to align our will to His."

—JOHN STOTT

"And when you pray, you must not be like the hypocrites. For they love to stand and pray in the synagogues and at the street corners, that they may be seen by others. Truly, I say to you, they have received their reward. But when you pray, go into your room and shut the door and pray to your Father who is in secret. And your Father who sees in secret will reward you. And when you pray, do not heap up empty phrases as the Gentiles do, for they think that they will be heard for their many words. Do not be like them, for your Father knows what you need before you ask him."

—JESUS, MATTHEW 6:5-8.

Why Do We Pray?

Why do we pray, anyway? Think of some of the prayers you may have learned as a child. *"Now I lay me down to sleep…"* or *"God is great, God is good"* come to mind. As we've previously discussed, many of us know the Lord's Prayer. If you're familiar with these prayers, you'll recall that in the first example, we ask God for something. In the second, we thank Him for something. And in the Lord's Prayer, Jesus suggests an outline of how to pray. But beyond asking for things or expressing gratitude, have you ever really thought about why we pray? Just what is prayer's purpose?

Perhaps it'll help if we think of what happens when we pray. There are at least three authentic outcomes of our prayer time with God.

Three Outcomes of Prayer

One | Conversation

Conversation occurs. Prayer is talking with God. He's a person. He is three persons (Father, Son, and Holy Spirit), and when we engage in prayer, we enjoy a close encounter, if you will, with the Godhead. It may seem like we do all the talking, but if, every once in a while, we take a breath and be still, we can gain a sense of His side of the conversation.

Two | Intimacy

Intimacy is fostered. Just like a conversation with our spouse, a parent, or a close friend promotes more in-depth levels of intimacy, dialogue with God can drive us to deeper levels of sharing. But this only happens when we take our interaction beyond simple facts and needs. We have to be honest and make ourselves vulnerable, which is not always easy! But we gain the most when we steer our conversation with the Father toward our deepest needs, desires, and emotions—communicating to God our very heart, soul, and mind.

Three | Change

Change happens. Whether we realize it or not, every encounter with God triggers some change in us—big or small—and, ultimately, all for good. It's a process of transformation that moves us closer and closer to fulfilling our potential as children of God. He is unchanging—His character, His attributes, His love for us wavers not one bit. So the change happens in us. This is the power of prayer. Sometimes the change is an immediate conviction prompting us to stop something, start something, or adjust an attitude of the heart. Sometimes the change is miraculous. Sometimes the change is slow, even subtle, and occurs over time. But we are never the same again.

Any way you slice it, prayer is a means of connecting us with the divine and supernatural—with God Himself. And the more often we do it, the abler we are to recognize His voice and discern His will.

Reflection & Mentorship

Begin

- We pray to converse, grow in intimacy, and be changed by God.

Unpack

- How often do you think most Christian men pray?
- Is prayer easy or hard for you? Why?

Inform

- Jesus said in the verses above, *"And when you pray, you must not be like the hypocrites. For they love to stand and pray in the synagogues and at the street corners, that they may be seen by others."* Why could praying in public be perceived as hypocritical?
- Why do we pray when God already knows what we want and need?
- Jesus suggests praying in secret. Why is this more authentic?

Land

- If you could change anything about your prayer pattern, what would it be?
- What steps do you need to take to change this?

Do

- Make the change needed to your prayer pattern this week.
- Try journaling your prayers a few days this week.
- Discuss the benefits of journaling your prayers with a friend or mentor.

Prayer: The Method

"Prayer is simply a two-way conversation between you and God."

—BILLY GRAHAM

"Then you will call upon me and come and pray to me, and I will hear you."

—JEREMIAH 29:12

What Is Prayer?

Prayer is conversing with God, plain and simple. As our heavenly Father, God wants us to talk to Him about anything, any time, any place, in any frame of mind. So why do we make it so complicated? Brothers, it doesn't have to be hard. Whether you're new to the faith, an old-timer, or somewhere in between, it never hurts to start with a few basics.

Four Steps to A Healthy Prayer Pattern

Let's begin with an easy way to remember some key ingredients to effective prayer: A.C.T.S. Not the New Testament book of Acts, but the acronym.

We have already briefly touched on this in a previous chapter. A.C.T.S stands for **adoration, confession, thanksgiving,** and **supplication.** Seem too formulaic? Hey – my perspective is that any tool we can use to promote and encourage one-on-one intimacy with our Father is a plus. Here's what A.C.T.S is all about:

One | Adoration

You express your adoration for God when you worship Him. You praise Him for His attributes and actions, for who He is and all He has done, is doing, and will do in your life. God enjoys hearing your praise!

> *"Praise the Lord! Praise the Lord, O my soul! I will praise the Lord as long as I live; I will sing praises to my God while I have my being"*

> —Psalm 146:1-2.

Two | Confession

God already knows, of course, when you've strayed a little or a lot, but to acknowledge it—to agree with God about your wrong attitudes and actions – is to open the door to freedom from guilt and shame. Express sorrow for what you've said, thought, or done that is not pleasing to Him. Pour out your regrets, seeking God's forgiveness. Know and believe in His forgiveness even when you don't feel it. When you confess your sins, you receive God's mercy and cleansing. Confession ushers in a humble heart of gratitude that removes any barriers blocking your communication with our merciful, loving Father.

> *"If we confess our sins, He is faithful and just to forgive us our sins and to cleanse us from all unrighteousness"*

> —1 John 1:9.

Three | Thanksgiving

Say *"thank you"* to God! After all, He took your place on the cross, paying for your sins so that you can live with Him forever in paradise. Because of Him, you hit the biggest jackpot ever, and He gives us His love, protection, and provision to boot. Exercise a stance of gratitude to the One who gives all good gifts. We can (and should!) thank Him for what He teaches us through our hardships too.

> *"I will offer to you the sacrifice of thanksgiving*
> *and call on the name of the Lord"*
>
> —Psalm 116:17.

Four | Supplication

Don't be shy. It's okay to pray for what you want and need—and for the needs of others—your family, friends, pastor, leaders, missionaries, government leaders, and persecuted Christians around the world. Ask God for wisdom in every area of your life. Ask for His daily guidance, for courage, hope, and opportunities to serve.

> *"Let your requests be made known to God"*
>
> —Philippians 4:6.

Never again do you need to say, *"I don't know what to pray."* Remember ACTS. I don't know who first thought it up, but many Christian brothers and sisters around the globe use it to make their prayer lives more meaningful and productive. It's a great start to a healthy pattern of prayer.

Reflection & Mentorship

Begin

- The A.C.T.S. method is one pattern for prayer that is well balanced and a good place to begin.

Unpack

- Do you have a well-balanced prayer time, or do you mostly just jump to supplication (asking God for things)?
- What do you try to do to regularly adore, confess, and give thanks in your prayers?

Inform

- When it says in Jeremiah 29:12, *"Then you will call upon me and come and pray to me, and I will hear you."* Do you believe this?
- How do you know when God has heard you? When God says in Scripture he has or only when he answers you?
- How has prayer strengthened your faith in God?

Land

- What issue do you have in praying and hearing answers?
- How could praying the A.C.T.S. method help?

Do

- Pray the A.C.T.S. method for one week.
- Report back to a friend or mentor the results of this prayer pattern on your relationship with God.

Prayer: The Lord's Prayer

"The great people of the earth today are the people
who pray."

—S.D. GORDON.

"Pray then like this..."

—JESUS, MATTHEW 6:9

Praying Like Jesus

The Lord's Prayer is a classic. Maybe you know it by heart. No worries if you don't, but a lot of folks do. The danger is that rote repetition can get in the way of remembering this elegant prayer's meaning and purpose. There's a reason it's called **The Lord's Prayer.** Jesus taught it to His disciples as an example not of what to pray, but of how to pray.

*"Pray then like this: Our Father in heaven, hallowed be your name.
Your kingdom come, your will be done, on earth as it is in heaven.
Give us this day our daily bread, and forgive us our debts, as we
also have forgiven our debtors. And lead us not into temptation, but
deliver us from evil."*

—Matthew 6:9-13

The 6 Building Blocks of The Lord's Prayer

So I count six building blocks to keep in mind while conversing with God.

Block One | "Our Father in heaven, hallowed be your name."

We acknowledge both our relationship with God (we are his children) and his authority. He reigns from heaven, and he is holy.

Block Two | "Your kingdom come."

We express grateful anticipation - the expectation that God's kingdom is at hand.

Block Three | "Your will be done, on earth as it is in heaven."

We reflect a desire for God's will to be accomplished—everywhere and in every situation.

Block Four | "Give us this day our daily bread."

Note that Jesus uses the word *"us."* We ask not only for our own needs but also the needs of others.

Block Five | "And forgive us our debts, as we also have forgiven our debtors."

We ask God to forgive us for our missteps, even as we double-check to make sure we've forgiven others who have wronged us.

Block Six | "And lead us not into temptation, but deliver us from evil."

We ask God to help us not sin and to protect us from injury, illness, or any other kind of harm. Note the plural language—*"our," "we," "us"*—the implication is that we can pray to God not only as individuals but also corporately with other believers.

Think of the Lord's Prayer essentially as an outline. Every portion can be expanded and personalized to reflect the specifics of your life, your family and friends, your wants and needs. God delights in hearing it all. So when you pray, carve out some time to be thorough. Here's what writer and speaker S. D. Gordon had to say about those who make prayer a priority:

> *"The great people of the earth today are the people who pray. I do not mean those who talk about prayer, but I mean those people who take time to pray. They have not time. It must be taken from something else. This something else is important, very important and pressing, but still less important and less pressing than prayer."*
>
> –S.D. Gordon

Just do it. Sit down with your heavenly Father and pour out your heart. You'll be blessed, and so will He.

Reflection & Mentorship

Begin

- Prayer is simply pouring our heart out before God, and Jesus taught us to pray like this—in full surrender to God.

Unpack

- Why is it special that Jesus teaches us how to pray?
- Do you think Jesus enjoyed teaching the disciples how to pray?
- What do you think was so mystifying about the way Jesus prayed that the disciples would ask him to teach them?

Inform

- In the Lord's Prayer above, what is your favorite verse? Why?
- What could be a challenging request in the Lord's Prayer?
- Have you ever prayed the Lord's Prayer in your own words?

Land

- What do you need to change about how you pray based on the teaching of the Lord's Prayer?

Do

- Act on this needed change this week.

Solitude: The Quiet Discipline

"Solitude is the furnace of transformation. Without solitude, we remain victims of our society and continue to be entangled in the illusions of the false self."

—HENRI NOUWEN

And he said to them, "Come away by yourselves to a desolate place and rest awhile." For many were coming and going, and they had no leisure even to eat.

—MARK 6:31

We have little of it

If there is one thing that our society has mass deficiencies in its solitude. Solitude is being alone and quiet so that we can contemplate. It demands freedom from the distractions of television, radio, devices, and other people. In solitude, we withdraw from the noise of life, engage reflective thought, war with personal failure, explore future options, and find direction from God.

Maybe we're trying to avoid it?

Most of us don't like the quietness of solitude. We have grown accustomed to the noise that fills our souls, consumes our minds, and drives our behaviors.

The static is not just coming from the devices we carry. It comes from the conversations, problems, meetings, sporting activities, and the flurry of family members traveling in competing directions all at the same time. Without knowing it, we have grown accustomed to the noise as if we need the stimulation. *"Stimulation"* not *"solitude"* is the theme that describes our lives.

Given the noise referenced above, why would we resist solitude when it appears we might be craving it? Maybe it's because being alone and uninterrupted is terrifying. In absolute quietness, we are forced to view the infrastructure we have built in our life. In solitude, we are forced to face issues we struggle with and have to be honest about regarding the state of our character, relationship, marriage, children, and work. In solitude, we encounter a God who wants to comfort and challenge us. In solitude, there is accountability with God who knows all and sees all. In solitude, our motives and desires are revealed, and we have to assess and evaluate them when the noise of the world allowed us to avoid them.

Yet a wise man is willing to look square in the eye of the infrastructure of their life rather than live with a lie. Great men are strong enough to withstand the silence and willing to confront the truth about themselves in the stillness of silence.

So what are the benefits of solitude?

Three Benefits of Solitude

One | In solitude, we are forged

No one wrote more eloquently on solitude than Henri Nouwen. He said, *"Solitude is the furnace of transformation. Without solitude, we remain victims of our society and continue to be entangled in the illusions of the false self."* Why is this? Because in solitude, we face the facts about ourselves, not the persona we seek to project or the person that others see and tend to believe. Isolation thus terrifies most men because it is the retreat toward reality. But it simultaneously beckons us because it's the voyage to transformation. It frightens us to reflect on the truth about our sinful nature, desires, and behaviors, but it equally invites us to know God more deeply and follow Him more intimately. In solitude, lies we have wrongly believed are displayed, discovered, disputed, and dismissed, and when combined with the truth of Scripture, they are defeated. Solitude thus becomes the furnace that men who need being refined, forged, and sharpened.

Two | In solitude, we hear the voice of God

The books of Kings have an intriguing encounter of man with God. Elijah the prophet was beat up, discouraged, and exhausted and went to a remote place where he found refuge in a cave and sought God. Here is the account:

> *"And [God] said, 'Go out and stand on the mount before the Lord.'*
> *And behold, the Lord passed by, and a great and strong wind tore*
> *the mountains and broke in pieces the rocks before the Lord, but*
> *the Lord was not in the wind. And after the wind an earthquake,*
> *but the Lord was not in the earthquake. And after the earthquake*
> *a fire, but the Lord was not in the fire. And after the fire*
> *the sound of a low whisper.'"*

—1 Kings 19:11-12.

A *"low whisper"* is how God chooses to speak us, but how do we hear that whisper in the noise of life? We usually don't, and it is why we often don't believe that God is still speaking today. He is, but we are often not able to hear him. If you desire to hear God's *"low whisper,"* get away and practice solitude.

Three | In solitude, we discover a divine relationship

"Be still, and know that I am God" declares Psalm 46:10. And it is in silence that we find the need for this "knowing." Knowing is not just an intellectual

exchange; it is intimacy with God found in silent communication. Like the intimacy we discover as we lie with a son or daughter in bed as they begin to drift to sleep—this child longs for the safety of closeness not found in verbal communication or recreational stimulation. This type of intimacy is only found in being close to God in the practice of solitude. For solitude is not about escaping to be alone—it's about escaping the noise to be alone *"with God,"* which might appear to others as escapism. But it's not isolation from God, only isolation from the things of this world.

In fact, the more intense our lives, the more we need those times of solitude. This is not a *"time out."* Instead, it's a time to be *"in."* It's a *"time in"* with God.

Reflection & Mentorship

Begin

- Solitude is our furnace of transformation; we should desire it and the relationship with God.

Unpack

- Do you think it's true that men are terrified of solitude?
- Have you ever practiced being alone with God? Is so, what was it like? If not, what has prevented you?

Inform

- What about Psalm 46:10, *"Be still, and know that I am God"* concerns you when you read these words?
- What does *"be still"* mean in your own words?
- What does *"know"* mean in your own words?

Land

- What needs to happen for you to find solitude?
- What steps can you take this week to try a short experience in solitude?

Do

- Practice a few minutes of solitude 1-2 times this week
- Report your experience with a friend or mentor.

Solitude: The Practice

Solitude is not something you must hope for in the future.
Instead, it is a deepening of the present, and unless
you look for it in the present you will
never find it.

—THOMAS MERTON

The Lord is my shepherd; I shall not want. He makes me lie
down in green pastures. He leads me beside still waters. He
restores my soul. He leads me in paths of righteousness
for his name's sake.

—KING DAVID IN PSALM 23:1-3

How Do I Begin?

think we can agree that practicing solitude is an essential tool in our spiritual transformation. As Thomas Merton said above, *"Unless you look for it in the present, you will never find it."* But often, the obstacle is merely knowing where to begin. Here's a primer for men who want to practice solitude but have never tried it before.

Seven Steps to Solitude

One | Find a time and place

For those who are new to the practice of establishing a time, I suggest an hour to begin, working your way up to a few hours, a half-day, or even a whole day. This needs to land on your calendar as a priority item on a monthly rotation if it's a one to three-hour time period or quarterly if it's a full day. But it can't be optional. If it's optional, you will allow it to be crowded out by other activities, which is the very reason so many people find it hard to practice (they never get around to it). Next, you need to find a place. It should be somewhere away from home (if possible) where you can be quiet and uninterrupted. Parks, lakes, libraries, cabins, monasteries, beaches, and the like are great places.

Two | Bring a Bible and a journal

Always bring these two tools. Your Bible, in physical form, not a Bible application on a device. Devices are full of entertainment, pop-ups, and messages that will only interfere with the process. The journal is for recording your thoughts as you navigate the time with God. Writing in silence is an excellent way of slowing our thoughts, marking conversations, scribing questions, and clearing your mind, heart, and soul of stimulations that have prevented quietness with the Lord. As you progress in practice, you will discover you want to focus on particular themes, so bringing other material may be desirable. Start with the basics and get to know the rhythm of the practice, since on a first pass it will be awkward.

Three | Kill all distractions

Turn off and even remove the mobile device. Be television free. Turn the music off. Be out of the vision of people. This is solitude. It's quiet and free from any distractions that would take your mind off the business at hand.

You are going to be initially distracted by the lack of stimulation anyway. Cheating on this is merely cheating yourself of purity in practice, and you might miss out on something significant.

Four | Talking, singing, praying, reading, and writing.

I bet you are saying, *"Whaaaat?"* I thought we were supposed to be completely silent. Yes and no. Solitude removes us from the distractions and stimulations of the world, but not from God. So feel free to talk, sing, and pray with him. Since no one is watching, do it out loud. We know Jesus did the same since others recorded many of his times of solitude.

The Beginning

You might want to start your time with a short prayer, again out loud, inviting God into this time and inviting him to speak—he is listening. While you are alone, God is going to be with you, and perhaps more intimate than you have experienced him ever in your life. Consider leaving a place for him to sit with you, and even imagine him with you. This might feel strange, but it's a spiritual reality.

The Middle

Next, take some time to read the Bible. You might consider being strategic in your reading by preparing text to meditate on during this time. If you came unprepared with books of the Bible to focus on, then go to the Psalms. Each Psalm has a different emphasis and theme, yet a rhythm conducive to solitude and reflection. As you read, stop and record your observations and thoughts in your journal. For example, when you feel convicted by a text, stop and journal about this conviction. When you feel inspired, stop and sing the Psalm (remember no one is listening to how bad your prose or voice is, and God doesn't care). When you feel remorse, stop and confess in prayer. Remember that God speaks in these low whispers. As you are inspired, reflect on where you have been over the last season and where you might want to go as a man of God—and write it in your journal. Write about misplaced desires and new godly desires you would like to fan into flame. Write about personal reformation you need in life, marriage, family, career, and calling. Having done this, take time to repent, seek forgiveness, and recommit to the Lord.

The End

Close the time with a look ahead. Consider what you desire to do differently as you move forward. Write it down, draw a picture, or bullet point a list of things. Be honest with yourself about what it will take for you to do your life differently. Accurate evaluation is the beginning of life transformation, but actionable steps build the bridge from a feeling of conviction to living with conviction. Don't allow yourself to pass over areas of your life that need immediate change. And don't minimize the steps you need to take in those areas.

Five | Make it concrete

Whether you are a writer or not, journaling your thoughts and observations as you have them, even in chaos and at random, is very beneficial. There is something concrete about putting words on paper that you can see. There is something about slowing your hand to write thoughts on a page. It also becomes a starting place for solitude when your next occasion rolls around on the calendar. It becomes a record of your life as you start to practice solitude regularly. You will look back over other entries and be amazed at what God has done in your life through this regular practice.

If you become sluggish or your mind wanders during the time, take a walk; enjoy God's creation and remember to listen. God speaks in a low whisper, so don't miss the details of the created order—the blowing of a breeze through the trees, wildlife running through a wooded park, the peaceful fall of snow in the winter, and the smells of a campfire, trees, or a nearby lake. Pay attention to a thought that demands your attention, even a metaphor that guides your reflection toward something profound and straightforward. These thoughts may well be the low whisper of God. Write it down and consider whether this is a message from God for only you. God regularly speaks to us, but we often don't hear because of the noise.

Six | Ask the hard questions

Times of solitude are the best times to ask the hard questions about our lives. Are my relationships the best? Have I made great decisions? Is my life aligned with godly values? Does my character need adjustment? Do I have an unaddressed sin issue? How's my marriage? How's my leadership? In all, you are considering what you need to do differently. Hard questions are the best questions because they drive to the core issue of our lives. As you ask those questions, record your thoughts and observations in your journal for future reference. Then pray through the answers you have written in your journal.

Seven | Commit to the next time

Last but not least, while you are still in the experience, commit on a calendar to the next time of solitude. Don't leave until the date is set and on your schedule.

Reflection & Mentorship

Begin

- Solitude is quiet practice, but we have to step ourselves through the process.

Unpack

- Which of the seven steps above seem the strangest or most

challenging?
- Have you tried any of these steps outside of solitude? If so, which ones?

Inform

- David said in Psalm 23:1-3, "*The Lord is my shepherd; I shall not want. He makes me lie down in green pastures. He leads me beside still waters. He restores my soul. He leads me in paths of righteousness for his name's sake.*" What are some key observations about solitude here, realizing David probably wrote this in solitude?

Land

- Where can you start with this practice?
- What do you want to focus on?

Do

- Set the calendar date and commit to it.

Prayer:
Bold, Persistent, and Faithful

"Bold prayers honor God, and God honors bold prayers. God isn't offended by your biggest dreams or boldest prayers. He is offended by anything less. If your prayers aren't impossible to you, they are insulting to God."

—MARK BATTERSON.

"And will not God give justice to his elect, who cry to him day and night? Will he delay long over them? I tell you, he will give justice to them speedily."

—LUKE 18:7-8

Stop being a prayer wimp

Are your prayers timid or bold? Do you pray with persistence or are you one and done? Do you pray for the impossible, or do you settle for the manageable stuff? Do you pray for situations that will challenge and excel your growth or only that which offers the status quo?

Three Actions That Will Increase the Strength of Your Prayers

One | Pray boldly

God commands us to pray bold, significant, and impossible prayers—for a physical illness, a wayward child, a declining marriage, an ongoing addiction, or a lingering pain from past injustice, it doesn't matter. God wants us to share, and God wants to hear it. How and when God chooses to answer us is his responsibility, ours is to pray and pray boldly. Even Jesus, when he was teaching the disciples to pray, dropped bold requests into his teaching. *"Your kingdom come, your will be done, on earth as it is in heaven"* is not a timid request. He modeled bold prayers. Even what is known as the High Priestly Prayer in the Gospel of John (John 17:1-26) is one of the most courageous prayers ever prayed, and Jesus prayed it. Here are a few lines from that prayer.

> *"I do not ask for these only, but also for those who will believe in me through their word, that they may all be one, just as you, Father, are in me, and I in you, that they also may be in us, so that the world may believe that you have sent me. The glory that you have given me I have given to them, that they may be one even as we are one, I in them and you in me, that they may become perfectly one, so that the world may know that you sent me and loved them even as you loved me."*
>
> —John 17:20-23

God is God, and we are not. He can do what we consider impossible. We cannot. Yet God invites our conversation and bold requests through our prayer and requests. He almost dares us to pray boldly. It may seem unnatural at first but embrace the audacity. God is not scared of it. He welcomes it.

Two | Pray persistently

In the gospel of Luke, Jesus shared a story, called a parable, which he told to help people understand the importance of persistent prayers, even when answers elude us. Here is how the story reads.

> He said, "In a certain city there was a judge who neither feared God nor respected man. And there was a widow in that city who kept coming to him and saying, 'Give me justice against my adversary.' For a while he refused, but afterward he said to himself, 'Though I neither fear God nor respect man, yet because this widow keeps bothering me, I will give her justice, so that she will not beat me down by her continual coming.' "And the Lord said, "Hear what the unrighteous judge says. And will not God give justice to his elect, who cry to him day and night? Will he delay long over them? I tell you, he will give justice to them speedily. Nevertheless, when the Son of Man comes, will he find faith on earth?"
>
> —Luke 18:2-8

What is the lesson in this but that our righteous God and good judge knows how to give good gifts to those who persist in their asking? What is required is not concern about the asking or concern about God's judgment, but rather a persistent prayer by a man of God. How long should we pray about an issue? Well, as long as it takes. If God put the burden on our heart, he wants us to pray persistently and not give up. As the last verse of the story points out, he wants to see our faith through our persistence in prayer.

Three | Pray faithfully

In the book of Mark, there is an account of a father who brought his son to Jesus. This son was under the possession of an evil spirit. Whenever it seized his son, it threw him to the ground. He foamed at the mouth, gnashed his teeth, and became rigid. His disciples had trouble healing him, and then Jesus responded:

> *"O faithless generation, how long am I to be with you? How long am I to bear with you? Bring him to me." And they brought the boy to him. And when the spirit saw him, immediately it convulsed the boy, and he fell on the ground and rolled about, foaming at the mouth. And Jesus asked his father, "How long has this been happening to him?" And he said, "From childhood. And it has often cast him into fire and into water, to destroy him. But if you can do anything, have compassion on us and help us." And Jesus said to him, "'If you can'! All things are possible for one who believes." Immediately the father of the child cried out and said, "I believe; help my unbelief!"*

> —Mark 9:19-24

This father reveals what the real challenge of faith looks like in prayer. He tells Jesus that he believes that the impossible can be done—which is why he brought his son to him for healing. At the same time, he admits that he still is aware of the gap of his faith and says to Jesus, *"I do believe [to some extent]; help me overcome [the extent of] my unbelief."*

All of us struggle at times with our belief about the things Jesus can or will do about things we ask in prayer. We walk the tightrope of human reasoning which teeters on the crazy proposition that God will act—this is a complete and active faith. But faith is found in overcoming our unbelief and learning to trust Him for the outcome, no matter how crazy the propositions in our prayer or how outrageous the circumstances.

What do you need?

If you need something, start to pray boldly, persistently, and faithfully. As you do, also pray for increasing boldness, persistence, and faith and increase your confidence in God, the object of our prayer. Building a relationship with God is the reason for the prayer, and prayer will always be an exercise in our relationship with Him. The more we practice bold, persistent, faithful praying, the stronger our relationship will be, which results in limitless possibilities.

Reflection & Mentorship

Begin

- As men, we need to pray more boldly, persistently, and faithfully.

Unpack

- Are you a prayer wimp? Yes or no. Why or why not?
- What tactics have you used to pray less wimpy prayers?

Inform

- Which of the three points above on bold, persistence, and faithfulness is convicting for you?

Land

- How can you pray more boldly?
- How can you pray more persistently?
- How can you pray more faithfully?

Do

- Take one action this week to pray stronger prayers and develop some spiritual muscle in your prayer time.
- Invite a friend or mentor to hold you accountable.

Finding Rest

"He who cannot rest, cannot work; he who cannot let go,
cannot hold on; he who cannot find footing,
cannot go forward."

—HARRY EMERSON FOSDICK

"Come to me, all who labor and are heavy laden, and I will
give you rest."

—JESUS, MATTHEW 11:28

We Live in A State of Constant Stress

If there is one word that could characterize most men's lives today, it would be—stress. We experience stress in our marriage, with our children, in our work, regarding the future, in self-imposed expectations, and I am sure you could add to this list different stresses you are currently experiencing. Pile on sin and the guilt that goes with it, and stress is compounded with a feeling of spiritual inadequacy.

But Jesus has been and always will be the answer to your burdens. In the Gospel of Matthew, he proclaims this charge.

> *"Come to me, all who labor and are heavy laden, and I will give you rest. Take my yoke upon you, and learn from me, for I am gentle and*

lowly in heart, and you will find rest for your souls. For my yoke is easy, and my burden is light."

—Matthew 11:28-30.

Three Invitations of Jesus

First | Jesus invites us to come with our burdens

There are few more comforting words than when Jesus invites us to, *"Come to [him] and [he] will give you rest."* If you've ever wanted to lay down your stresses, anxieties, worries, fears, or frustrations, this is a welcomed invitation. For the burdens you experience can be far more substantial than any physical load you have carried. They accompany you everywhere—to work, in recreation, in bed at night, and often they get in the way of relationships and needed rest. While there are vices you can turn to for temporary relief, the burdens you experience demand a strong prescription that only Jesus can provide.

Coming to him with your stresses, anxieties, worries, fears, frustrations, and all of your burdens allows him to bear under the weight of them since he is the only one who can, has, and can extend the rest you need under this load. This is an invitation by him to lay your burdens down before him and to rid yourself of the weight you have been lugging around.

Second | Jesus invites us to take on a different yoke

Jesus continues, *"Take my yoke upon you, and learn from me, for I am gentle and lowly in heart, and you will find rest for your souls."* Giving your burdens to Him comes with an invitation to let go of worldly burdens and take on a different *"yoke"* or *"burden"*—the burden of following him. The literal yoke inferred here is the yoke that is placed on cattle when they plow a field. It is a reference to being bound to following Jesus and therefore yielding to his guidance, direction, and leadership of your life. While this burden is a different yoke, it has a different *"weight,"* one that seeks your best for a fruitful life. He invites us to take on his yoke and subsequently *"learn from"* him. It is to learn a take on a new burden, one that provides us soul rest through this life. It is one with a fresh perspective, worldview, and insight only discovered as we yield to his direction and guidance, which results in a lighter burden.

Why should you trust him? Because he is *"gentle and lowly in heart."* Often your notions about what Jesus is like are not only incorrect, but they are turned upside. You will be tempted to view God as *harsh, distant, condemning, punitive, or unsympathetic,* but these are false assumptions. God is not a killjoy but rather a joy-giver. And while there is a burden to bear, Jesus bore the burden for you on the cross. And the reward for believers is burdens lifted. It is something we learn in the wearing of his yoke—that Jesus' direction is gentle and caring. Jesus implores you. He says:

> *My kindness will overwhelm you.*
> *My gentleness will surprise you.*
> *My humility will draw you to me.*
> *My forgiveness will cover all your sin.*
> *My compassion will surround you*
> *And you will find rest for your souls.*

All of us bear some burden, which is the yoke we carry, even if we are burdened with self. None of these yokes compare to the yoke of Jesus, and he is the only one who can bring rest to your souls. If your weight is too heavy, try to bear his yoke.

Third | Jesus invites us to let go of fear

There are many reasons not to exchange our other yokes for the yoke of Jesus, but the most significant reason is fear. This leads to numerous questions, such as:

Can I trust that God has my best interests in mind?
Will He ask of me something that I don't want to do?
Will I have to give up too much of my freedom?
Will he truly be good to me?

All of these kinds of questions you wrestle with come down to one thing—fear. And Jesus understands your worries and assures you, *"For my yoke is easy, and my burden is light."* But how can this be possible? It's possible because when you wear his yoke, you don't carry your burdens anymore, rather, Jesus does. He willingly takes them when you willingly give them daily as you cast all your cares upon him, and he carries them for you. Furthermore, when you wear his yoke, you don't do it alone but with the help of the Holy Spirit—God Himself who is resident in our hearts and empowers us for life and godliness.

Ultimately, his burden is different or *"light"* because everything that he teaches you to do is always for your good. Always. Living His way leaves us with a load lifted, a clean conscience, and a life well-lived.

Have you laid your burdens down, taken up his yoke, and found rest for your soul?

Reflection & Mentorship

Begin

- Jesus invites us to soul rest, which requires exchanging heavy burdens for lighter ones.

Unpack

- What do most men fret about on a regular basis?
- What one thing is a burden to you right now?

- Would you like to be free of this burden? What is keeping you from letting go of this burden?

Inform

- When Jesus says, *"Take my yoke upon you,"* does this sound like more to burden you?
- In contrast, Jesus also says, *"For my yoke is easy, and my burden is light."* How does this alter how you feel about a relationship with Jesus?

Land

- Do you believe following Jesus is more burden or rest? Is there a difference?
- What do you need to be praying for that is a burden you would like to have lifted?
- What action do you need to take to release these burdens?

Do

- Take action on giving up burdens this week to Jesus.
- Lay them down and avoid picking them back up.
- Report back to a friend or a mentor why it was hard to avoid *"bearing up under"* these burdens again.

Keeping Peace

"When the power of love overcomes the love of power,
the world will know peace."

—JIMI HENDRIX

"Blessed are the peacemakers, for they shall be called
sons of God."

—JESUS, MATTHEW 5:9

Relationships Require Peace Because They Are Valuable

Relationships are valuable in life. They are challenging to construct and easy to deconstruct. There are so many ways to sabotage your relationships. Here are some behaviors to keep your relationships from being compromised and help maintain peace with those around you.

8 Behaviors to Avoid to Keep Peace

One | Triangulation rather than directly addressing

Triangulation occurs when you share your issues about another person with anyone other than that individual. What you have done is to bring another into what is your perceived issue and often into an alliance with you against others. This does not solve the problem but enlarges the circle of conflict with individuals who were not part of the original dispute and who have no influence to resolve the conflict. The uninvolved party you've brought in now have a bias about the person you have a dispute with but without a way to resolve that bias since the issue is yours rather than theirs.

Two | Carbon copying emails to uninvolved people

Of course, once you carbon copy anyone they become involved. This is usually a power play or a move to bring others over to your side, but it results in nothing good besides enlarging the circle of mistrust and doubt. Remember that the larger the circle of people involved—passively or actively—the harder it is to resolve conflict. If your goal is to preserve relationships, you will resist any actions that needlessly widen the circle.

Three | Sharing second-hand information as factual

Second-hand information is not usually actual information. At best, it is highly suspect because as second-hand information, you don't know all the facts. There is no reason to share second- or third-hand information if you care about others. It's no different from gossip. Often, others don't need to know, and you usually don't have a good reason to share what you do know or have heard.

Four | Escalating small issues into more significant conflict

When small disagreements are left unresolved, they have the opportunity to grow into more significant conflicts. Keeping short accounts with others is the key to keeping little things from escalating into more significant misunderstandings. As Scripture teaches, if you have an offense against a brother, go immediately to that brother and settle your account. It does not matter if you were responsible for the initial disagreement or your friend. You are responsible to act on the conviction. Go and resolve it quickly.

Five | Ignoring issues that you should address

Some who are conflict-averse fail to deal with issues they know are problematic and, therefore, allow the dysfunctions to spill into the life of others. This is the source of much pain on teams, in organizations, within families, and in churches. When we choose not to confront issues, behaviors, or problems, they will have a detrimental impact on people.

Six | Failing to communicate the loving truth

Truth should be shared graciously and only with the right people, but if you have issues, you need to share those issues in truth and love. Many relationships have failed because of sheltering people from the truth or communicating half-truths because someone did not dare to be forthcoming. If you truly love someone, you will tell them the truth—not a half-truth or a lie to avoid friction or pain. Avoidance of sharing the truth always leads to more significant conflict in the future.

Seven | Demonizing those who disagree with you

Have you ever met people who are your best friend until you disagree with them on some issue and then you become an enemy? It happens all the time. You will be tempted to divide the world into good people and bad people or righteous and unrighteous. Life isn't that easy. Besides, which group would you be in? Good and godly people can do and say unfortunate things, and they can disagree with your opinions, but you should never demonize them for doing so. Healthy individuals give others space and allow them to disagree without the friendship being threatened.

Eight | Owning other people's issues

This is another form of triangulation. Your problems are yours, and my issues are mine. I can give you counsel or take your counsel, but the issues are still either mine or yours. If I take up your problem or get involved in a conflict that is not my own, I cannot truly resolve it. We may do this out of love, but it doesn't work and frequently produces escalating conflict. Rather than taking up the issue of another, offer to mediate and see if peace can be found.

Jesus commanded us to be peacemakers. That starts with those closest to us by not allowing issues to cloud our friendships. And where we see that happen, whether it's us with us or others, let's us step in as peacemakers on behalf of Jesus.

Reflection & Mentorship

Begin

- Keeping peace can be hard but there are certain behaviors we can avoid.

Unpack

- I am sure you know argumentative people. What tactics do they use to get their way?
- How is *"power play"* and *"control"* a big part of arguments?

Inform

- Of the eight points above, which ones are you currently encountering? Explain the situations without naming people.
- When Jesus says, *"Blessed are the peacemakers, for they shall be called sons of God,"* why would peacemakers be called *"sons of*

God?" How is peacemaking in alignment with the identity of a godly representative?

Land

- Of the eight points above, which do you have the tendency to perpetuate?
- What issues do you need to address immediately?
- What steps do you need to take to keep peace?

Do

- Take action on keeping peace with others.
- Embrace the challenge of taking peaceful action even when others push toward arguments and fights?
- Over the next week, share with a friend or a mentor about the challenges you have faced in attempting to keep peace with others.

Trusting God

"Having thus chosen our course, without guile and with
pure purpose, let us renew our trust in God, and go forward
without fear and with manly hearts."

—ABRAHAM LINCOLN

"Blessed is the man who trusts in the Lord,
whose trust is the Lord."

—JEREMIAH 17:7

Great Men Trust in a Great God

You'll hear Christians say, sometimes tritely, *"Just trust in God."* We should trust Him in all things, but what does that mean? How do you do it?

The prophet Jeremiah speaks to this matter of trust in Jeremiah 17:5-10. He breaks the issue of trust down to its essential elements. He was driven to trust God in changing times and trusted Him when others didn't. So let's discover the wisdom of a man who was deeply challenged to trust God and saw its result.

Growing Trust of God

First | The wrong place to focus your trust

> *Thus says the Lord: "Cursed is the man who trusts in man and makes flesh his strength, whose heart turns away from the Lord. He is like a shrub in the desert, and shall not see any good come. He shall dwell in the parched places of the wilderness, in an uninhabited salt land."*

> —Jeremiah 17:5-6

The wrong place to put your trust is in yourselves or other people. Notice the sharp language that Jeremiah uses—*"Cursed is the man who trusts in man"* because in doing so, his *"heart turns away from the Lord."* As followers, you have given up the control of your lives to God, so to trust in yourself, your plans, and your schemes is not only foolishness, it's a rejection of the God who owns your lives, who wants to direct your paths and use you for His purposes. If you now belong to Him but are trusting in yourself, you're actively rejecting God's rightful ownership of your life.

The result is that you will not see the prosperity and blessing that God has for your life. He likens those who trust in themselves to a *"bush in the wastelands,"* who *"will not see prosperity"* but rather dwell in a parched place *"where no one lives."* It's a picture of living alone and without blessing, because you're living without the direction of God.

Second | The right place to focus your trust

> *"Blessed is the man who trusts in the Lord, whose trust is the Lord. He is like a tree planted by water, that sends out its roots by the stream, and does not fear when heat comes, for its leaves remain green, and is not anxious in the year of drought, for it does not cease to bear fruit."*

> —Jeremiah 17:7-8

Contrast the description we have of the one who trusts in himself with verses 7 and 8 regarding the blessings you'll experience in believing in the Lord and putting your confidence in him. God is saying, *"You can trust in yourself and live in the wasteland by yourself, missing my blessings, or you can choose to believe in me and live a blessed life like a tree planted by the water, its leaves always green and without the fear of drought."* That is a huge contrast in how you live life and how you'll experience the fullness of life.

Your sovereign Father knows what is best for you. He knows what you don't know about the circumstances of your lives. He knows the precise date of your last breath. He knows what life will look like tomorrow. He is also the one who can deal with issues of life which seem impossible for you. You like to control your destiny; however, you have very little control, if any, especially as a follower (note: *"follower"* is the operative word). God, on the other hand, can guide, direct your paths, remove barriers in your way, and give you favor with those you interact with. The bottom line, says Jeremiah, is that if you want a life that is all it can be, put your trust in God rather than in yourself.

Three | Be discerning about where your trust is placed.

> *"The heart is deceitful above all things, and desperately sick; who can understand it? I the Lord search the heart and test the mind, to give every man according to his ways, according to the fruit of his deeds."*
>
> —Jeremiah 17:9-10

Now you may well be saying, *"Of course I trust in God."* Great. How often do we make our plans and then only ask God to bless, protect, and ensure those plans? That is entirely different from asking Him to give you direction and guidance in the plan itself. Or permit Him to actually give you a plan in the first place.

Jeremiah reminds us that your hearts are deceitful above all things and that the Lord searches your heart, examines your mind, and rewards you accordingly. Wise men are discerning about their motivations and the true desires of their hearts. They can distinguish between trusting themselves and trusting God. They see every new day as a day to put their confidence in God rather than in themselves.

Another well-known proverb puts it this way:

> *"Trust in the Lord with all your heart, and do not lean on your own understanding. In all your ways acknowledge him, and he will make straight your paths."*

> —Proverbs 3:5-6

Reflection & Mentorship

Begin

- Growing in trusting God is not easy, but it is the path to wisdom and is vital in a growing relationship with God.

Unpack

- Do you think men remain in infant stages in their relationship with God? Why or why not?
- How is trust an activator of growth in a relationship with God?

Inform

- Which of these verses stood out to you?
- *Thus says the Lord: "Cursed is the man who trusts in man and makes flesh his strength, whose heart turns away from the Lord. He is like a shrub in the desert, and shall not see any good come. He shall dwell*

in the parched places of the wilderness, in an uninhabited salt land."
—Jeremiah 17:5-6

- *"Blessed is the man who trusts in the Lord, whose trust is the Lord. He is like a tree planted by water, that sends out its roots by the stream, and does not fear when heat comes, for its leaves remain green, and is not anxious in the year of drought, for it does not cease to bear fruit."*
  —Jeremiah 17:7-8
- *"The heart is deceitful above all things, and desperately sick; who can understand it? I the Lord search the heart and test the mind, to give every man according to his ways, according to the fruit of his deeds."*
  —Jeremiah 17:9-10
- What is the driving point of the text you selected?

Land

- What trust challenges do you encounter?
- What strides do you need to take to trust God more?
- How could a friend or mentor help?

Do

- Be more trusting by acting in trust this week.
- Share the results with a friend, family member, or mentor.

Leading Anger

Anybody can become angry—that is easy, but to be angry with the right person and to the right degree and at the right time and for the right purpose, and in the right way—that is not within everybody's power and is not easy.

—ARISTOTLE

Therefore, having put away falsehood, let each one of you speak the truth with his neighbor, for we are members one of another. Be angry and do not sin; do not let the sun go down on your anger, and give no opportunity to the devil. Let the thief no longer steal, but rather let him labor, doing honest work with his own hands, so that he may have something to share with anyone in need. Let no corrupting talk come out of your mouths, but only such as is good for building up, as fits the occasion, that it may give grace to those who hear. And do not grieve the Holy Spirit of God, by whom you were sealed for the day of redemption. Let all bitterness and wrath and anger and clamor and slander be put away from you, along with all malice. Be kind to one another, tenderhearted, forgiving one another, as God in Christ forgave you.

—EPHESIANS 4:25-32

Prone to anger?

So many men I know are prone to anger. In fact, many men of the Bible have inflicted grave injury on others in their rage. Moses is a prime example. In passion, he stepped in over his concern for the mistreatment of his fellow Hebrews. Yet his untamed passion brewed into a physical act of anger that resulted in homicide—in much the same way Cain acted with Able at the beginning of the Bible. And again later, when Moses was leading the people into the promised land, God instructed him to speak to the rock and God would open a river of water for his thirsty and obstinate people. Moses, however, in frustration, struck the rock over the criticisms of the Hebrews. He was right to be passionate but wrong to not control his holy dissatisfaction, which resulted in disobedience to God. Because of that one moment of defiant anger, he prevented by God from leading the people into the promised land.

In Cain's situation, his anger originated from misplaced selfishness and jealousy that resulted in violence. In Moses' case, he had a right to be angry, but his unchecked passion led to reckless fury. I am sure you can identify, as we have all been guilty of the same—including posts that should not have been shared, emails that should not have been sent, or words that should never have been spoken. And there are even a few of us who have acted violently, inflicting unjust physical injury on others.

So what can we learn?

Two Non-negotiables Regarding Anger

One | Anger is not wrong

> *"Be angry and do not sin; do not let the sun go down on your anger, and give no opportunity to the devil."*
>
> —Ephesians 4:26-27

It's clear from many biblical texts that anger is not wrong. God himself expressed anger through many Old Testament prophets who he used to rebuke individuals to entire nations for sin—for example, Sodom and Gomorrah. Or consider the perpetual evil of mankind, which resulted in a worldwide flood, wiping out corruption except for a single faithful family—for example, Noah and the great flood. God justly hates evil and wickedness. And we, too, should know God's holy anger—but we must moderate this because we do not act from a position of perfect love, holiness, and righteousness like God.

Unfortunately, it not righteous anger that usually gets us into trouble. When our anger is lit, it becomes a destructive wildfire around issues that are far more personal and typically surrounds our loss of control. It's sparked when a child tests a boundary we have set. It burns into flame when we feel we are losing in discussion with our spouse. It ignites when a colleague at work takes credit for what we have done. The problem is that, if unchecked, our initial anger will burn into full flame, and then words and actions are used to inflict burning pain, which damages relationships. Frequently, it is those we love most who experience the results of the anger we carry inside.

Two | Anger can result in wrongdoing

"Give no opportunity to the devil."

—Ephesians 4:27

Anger is a primary human emotion that all of us experience. It's a normal human reaction to everyday annoyances. However, how we handle our anger makes all the difference in the world. Unmoderated anger leads to unhealthy and often sinful actions, so our challenge is to bring our passion under control—or it might be better stated—under God's control. The following are five essential practices for us to keep our anger under His control.

First | Wait

Don't feel the need to act immediately. There are a few situations that require immediate action, like a life-threatening situation, but for all others, wait. Wait to respond until you have regained full access to your mental facilities, when your emotions, tone, and temperament are under control. Like Paul says in the verse above, *"Be angry and do not sin."* Paul is giving an allowance to anger but not the activity of the anger. The only way to do this is to wait to respond until you can do so in a measured and wise way.

Second | Keep short accounts

In the same verse, Paul says, *"Do not let the sun go down on your anger."* Addressing the issue as soon as it is possible is of vast importance. This is especially true in covenantal relationships, like in a marriage, a family, or in a church, where unresolved anger can lead to secrecy, resentment, bitterness, and conflict that prevents oneness. Many couples believe the application of this verse is literal, meaning two parties in disagreement don't sleep until the issue is resolved. While the application is not a bad practice, it may not be necessary. Learning to address the problem rather than bury it is the principle of the text—which means the short accounting method is excellent when it comes to matters of disagreement.

Third | Forgive

In Ephesians 4:32, Paul instructs us to *"Be kind to one another, tenderhearted, forgiving one another, as God in Christ forgave you."* The longer you hold on to unforgiveness, the less kind and tender you become to others. Unforgiveness is a prison that robs many of real joy. The irony is that the longer we hold on to it, the more it shackles us. Often, the other party is entirely unaware of our issues; therefore, the only person we are binding is ourselves. Consequently, we hold on to unforgiveness at our peril, but when we learn to forgive, we become like Christ, who demonstrated complete forgiveness.

Fourth | Lean on the Spirit

Invite the Holy Spirit to help you. He dwells within you and is your counselor, teacher, and helper. It is hard to stay angry when we invite the Spirit to help, convict, guide, and direct. Jesus said in John 16:8, *"And when [the Spirit] comes, he will convict the world concerning sin and righteousness and judgment."* Admittedly, there are deep wounds that need time and help to deal with, but in all cases, the Holy Spirit lives within us and will direct us toward right and righteousness.

Fifth | Practice fruitful engagement

Memorize and practice the fruit of the Holy Spirit, especially in situations where you are angry or irritated. Leaning on the products that come from being connected to the Spirit helps you know when you are out of step with God's way. Allow the fruit to become your plumb line, and when you are out-of-line, let the Spirit guide you back. *"But the fruit of the Spirit is love, joy, peace, patience, kindness, goodness, faithfulness, gentleness, self-control; against such things there is no law"*—Galatians 5:22-23. While everyone is prone to moments of anger, don't let your anger control you, but instead, be controlled by the Spirit.

Reflection & Mentorship

Begin

- Everyone experiences anger, but it's how we respond to our feelings of anger that makes the difference between it becoming sinful action or simply an indicator that something is wrong.

Unpack

- How have you recently been the victim of someone's anger? How did this feel and what was the impact?
- Have you recently acted in anger? Was it justifiable anger? Was your response appropriate or not? Do you wish you would have handled it differently?

Inform

- How is it possible to *"Be angry and do not sin,"* as Paul says in Ephesians 4:26?
- Galatians 5:22-23 reads, *"But the fruit of the Spirit is love, joy, peace, patience, kindness, goodness, faithfulness, gentleness, self-control; against such things there is no law."* Which fruit is challenging for you when you are angry?

Land

- How do you typically express anger?
- What regular moments bring out anger?
- How can you plan to act differently than you have in the past when these moments arise?

Do

- Work to moderate your anger by deploying one principle you discussed today.
- Enlist a brother to support you with advice.

Battling Sin

"I would rather die than do something which I know to be
a sin, or to be against God's will."

—JOAN OF ARC

"Are we to continue in sin that grace may abound?
By no means!"

—ROMANS 6:1-2

We Must Engage the Battle Even When the War Is Won

The war is on. The enemy is relentless, and fight we must. I'm talking about our battle with sin. True, Jesus paid for all our sins—past, present, and future—when he took our place on the cross. But, need I say it, his greatest sacrifice in no way gives us the license to keep sinning.

On the contrary, Jesus is our example of the ultimate man fully engaged in battle until his final breath. Fully divine and fully human, he remained sinless in the struggle—unlike us.

We battle with sin in our lives for many good reasons. We fight because we love Jesus. We fight to be credible witnesses to the world of His love for one and all. We fight to war with apathy, shame, and fear. And we fight it so that we can draw ever closer to the battle that Jesus fought for us. But we never fight to earn our salvation—that's Jesus' battle. And he fought and won.

Here's the tricky part. The battle is not purely physical, fought against people that we see. In fact, we don't fight it with guns, swords, bows, and fists at all. The battle is spiritual. So we must learn to fight differently yet at the same time be active and intentional about our battle plan. We can start by identifying the three battles of sin so we can *know the enemy* and strategize accordingly.

Three Battles We Fight

One | We Battle with Our Hurts

Nobody's perfect. Even our most beloved family members and closest friends let us down on occasion—sometimes inflicting wounds that run deep and linger long. Oh, how it can hurt. And sometimes we want to nurse the hurt and hold a grudge. But even the Lord's Prayer reflects Jesus' desire, in His typically radical, counter-culture way, that we do the opposite

*"…and forgive us our sins as we forgive those
who have sinned against us."*

So who in your life, have you not yet forgiven? While it might be easier (or dare we say *lazier*) to continue living imprisoned to the sin of unforgiveness, Jesus wants us to battle it by extending to others the forgiveness, love, grace, and mercy that he has shown to us.

Two | We Battle with Our Habits

What regular, repeated behavior patterns do you need to address?

Familiar to many of us are bad habits that do harm in some way both to us and to others, like greed, selfishness, overconsumption, offensive language, joking at another's expense, hurtful sarcasm, smoking, pornography—the list could go on, but I just bet you've already recognized yourself in there somewhere. Following Christ, however, means conquering these habits and developing new ones in their place. We need habits that build our character and establish the kind of virtue in our lives that truly reflect who Jesus is to the rest of the world.

Three | We Battle with Our Hang-ups

Some things in life stop us cold. They are blockades that seem impossible to get past, personal fixations that keep us from moving forward and going all in. We all get hung up on something. Maybe it's a family of origin pattern of behavior or personal insecurity that has embedded itself assumptively into our everyday lives. But, in Christ, we are overcomers. As children of God, we have access to His strength. With the help of the Holy Spirit, we can navigate these minefields and emerge victoriously.

You Don't Battle Alone

We are not alone in our battle against sin. The Father, Son, and Holy Spirit have our back. Our pride (now there's a weighty sin topic) must not convince us that we can wage and win this war on our power. Be warned—it's a daily, ongoing fight, but we must not surrender to defeat when occasionally we stumble. Our only surrender is to Jesus Christ Himself. We submit to Him, and in the end, his victory is ours. Guaranteed.

> *"Finally, be strong in the Lord and in the strength of His might. Put on the whole armor of God, that you may be able to stand against the schemes of the devil."*
>
> —Ephesians 6:10-11.

Reflection & Mentorship

Begin

- Men need to battle, but not against people—rather with our hurts, habits, and hang-ups.

Unpack

- Jesus won the war on sin—how does this make you feel? Strong? Certain? Victorious?
- Since so many men feel beat up by sin, do we merely forget this?

Inform

- Paul said in Romans 6:1-2, *"Are we to continue in sin that grace may abound?"* Why would someone sin to increase grace?
- Does anything *"increase"* God's grace? Or is there something faulty with this thinking?

Land

- What do you battle with more—hurts, habits, or hang-ups? Describe in detail.
- What steps do you need to battle more effectively with this challenge?

Do

- Engage the battle this week.
- Enlist a brother to support you in this battle.

Discerning Truth

"We need discernment in what we see and what we hear
and what we believe."

—CHARLES SWINDOLL

"And it is my prayer that your love may abound more and
more, with knowledge and all discernment, so that you may
approve what is excellent, and so be pure
and blameless for the day of Christ."

—PHILIPPIANS 1:9-10

Take a discernment test

Take a few minutes and read over the following statements. For each statement, consider if the statement is **true** or **false**.

1. The Bible contains truths but also mistakes that make it inaccurate and culturally irrelevant, so it cannot be trusted for providing relevant truth.
2. There are many paths to heaven; therefore, beliefs from other religions should be incorporated in developing a holistic and complete worldview.
3. A loving God would never send anyone to hell for eternity.

4. We are born into this world inherently good; we are not sinful, as some suggest from birth.

5. Jesus did not perform real miracles—for example, turning water to wine, healing the blind, or raising himself from the dead. These so-called miracles are only stories that gained acceptance over time by a few followers.

6. There is no historical evidence that holds any merit that Jesus rose from the dead.

7. When we get to heaven, Jesus will weigh our good deeds against our bad ones to determine whether we will gain entry.

8. The Bible states that *"God helps those who help themselves."*

9. God promises to relieve us of suffering in this life if we have enough faith.

10. There is little to no archeological evidence of biblical accounts found in the Middle East.

How many statements did you identify as true and how many as false? The reality is that every one of these ten statements is false. Not even one of them is bears any truth. But do you know how to spot actual evidence versus those that are fake?

How to Spot the Truth

First | Learn the genuine article

All of us grow up believing something—correct or not. At first, we blindly believe, merely accepting what we are taught as children. Over time, as we physically age and intellectually mature, the data we take in grows and the thoughts we have about life, work, and faith gain independence from our family of origin. At this point, we form personal judgments about the world. Over a lifetime, we construct large clusters of these beliefs, images, and ideas called a belief system or worldview. Unless you are aware of what is the truth and what is not, you can form entire systems of belief around wrong ideas (untruths) that others attempt to perpetuate. Many become blind to these accepted untruths and form biases that sometimes go unchallenged due to emotional attachments to them.

Consider for a moment how the Federal Bureau of Investigation prepares people to spot counterfeit currency. As they train one to have an eye for fakes, they do not exclusively show them counterfeit bills. In fact, they primarily show them authentic currency and train them to spot the characteristics of the real thing—not fakes. As they become increasingly intimate with the genuine product, they know when they spot an ungenuine product.

The same is true when it comes to your faith. When you read or hear something that is not true, like the statements above, there ought to be some recognition or even concern that what is being communicated might contain a falsehood or a manipulated truth. However, you will only notice this if you are a student of the genuine product. Notice what the apostle Paul says to his protégé, Timothy.

"But as for you, continue in what you have learned and have become convinced of, because you know those from whom you learned it, and how from infancy you have known the Holy Scriptures, which are able to make you wise for salvation through faith in Christ Jesus. All Scripture is God-breathed and is useful for teaching, rebuking, correcting, and training in righteousness, so that the servant of God may be thoroughly equipped for every good work."

— 2 Timothy 3:14-17.

As Paul suggests, the better we know the genuine article—scriptural truth—the better we know God himself and his salvation. As we get to know what God says, we will also know when we are being sold a *"fake bill"* of goods. When we start a relationship with God, regardless of our physical age, we are turning our lives and futures over to him and his way. It only makes sense that we consistently discover what God has to say and allow his truth to teach, rebuke, correct, and train us in his righteousness. We then need to not only accept these beliefs but to be able to explain these truths in sensible ways to those around us whose information about God is far from reality. We need to know the truth, live it, and explain it. That starts with becoming a student of His book—the Bible.

Second | Trust credible historical evidence

Christians who study the ancient proof supportive of Christianity are continually amazed at what they find. One distinctive of our faith is that it is rooted in history with real people, real situations, real places, and actual events. This is not a faith based on myths constructed in the distant past but concrete evidence based in a reasonable faith rooted in history—not fake news. Consider the following:

- Archeologists are continually finding new evidence of the accounts we read of in the Old Testament. Yes, constantly. And while pop media is not talking about it, in the last few decades, we have discovered tens of thousands of artifacts that support the writings of the Bible. While we don't have evidence for every story in the Bible, archeological finds are not contradicting the Bible.

- Historical accounts from other people groups such as Egyptians, Romans, and Greeks, align with biblical accounts. For instance, the forced exile of the Jews by Nebuchadnezzar as well as their repatriation by Cyrus is found in extra-biblical historical records. Even contemporary historians in Jesus' day reference Jesus and His followers for their care of the poor, elderly and needy, as well as their willingness to die for their beliefs.

- Even the evidence for the resurrection is overwhelming. As Chuck Colson said, *"If a few burglars could not keep Watergate a secret, how could twelve apostles fake the accounts of the resurrection and then all die for their faith."*

Some don't like the fact that the historical record is accurate, so they refuse to believe it and find every evidence possible that points to disproving its credibility and reliability. Ironically, a good historian generally believes what they observe from ancient sources unless they can find evidence that proves it to be false. This alone is an insightful twist, and thus, it becomes even more important for believers to know the reasons for Christianity's reliability. Because you will eventually be challenged, and we ought to know the best evidence and answers. Or at minimum, be given a chance to find them.

Third | Read and strengthen your apologetics

Wikipedia defines apologetics this way: *"Apologetics (from Greek, "speaking in defense") is the religious discipline of defending religious doctrines through systematic argumentation and discourse. Early Christian writers (c. 120–220) who defended their beliefs against critics and recommended their faith to outsiders were called Christian apologists."*

As Christ followers, we ought to be able to defend our faith and have a reasoned discussion with others. Here are some great books that may help you begin your journey:

- *Mere Christianity*, C. S. Lewis
- *Evidence that Demands a Verdict*, Josh McDowell
- *The Reason for God*, Timothy Keller
- *The Case for Christ*, Lee Strobel

Reflection & Mentorship

Begin

- A discerning man is a wise man.

Unpack

- Are older men naturally wiser than younger men?
- How is discernment related to wisdom?

Inform

- Paul said in Philippians 1:9-10, *"And it is my prayer that your love may abound more and more, with knowledge and all discernment, so that you may approve what is excellent, and so be pure and blameless for the day of Christ."* Does this mean we can grow in discernment?
- What factor contributes to discernment in these verses?
- What outputs does discernment produce?

Land

- Where do you need more discernment?
- What action do you need to take to increase your discernment?

Do

- Invite a friend or mentor to pray for your discernment.

ALSO BY VINCE MILLER

THIRTY VIRTUES THAT BUILD A MAN:
A Conversational Guide for Mentoring Any Man

Men are a strategic force for change in the world, but they have an enemy, and it's not what you think. It's apathy. It is the appeal of inaction that lives within every man's heart.

Thirty easy-to-use lesson guides are perfect for men of all ages to use in private reflection or mentoring conversation with other men.

$10.99 paperback

96 pages

ISBN: 978-1-946453-31-0

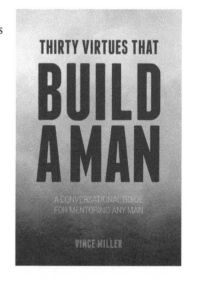

https://beresolute.org/product/thirty-virtues-that-build-men/

20 LESSONS THAT BUILD A LEADER:
A Conversational Mentoring Guide

Mentorship is something many of us seek—but many of us feel unqualified to be a mentor of others.

This book includes 20 simple lessons that not only teach fundamental leadership lesson but empower a mentor with conversation that take the guesswork of mentoring other.

$10.99 paperback

96 pages

ISBN: 978-1-946453-63-1

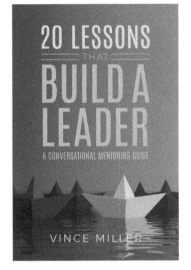

https://beresolute.org/product/twenty-lessons-that-build-a-leader/

20 LESSONS THAT BUILD A MAN'S FAMILY:
A Conversational Mentoring Guide

Being the husband, father, and leader your family needs is one of the great challenges you'll face as a man. It will test you to the core. And it will make you, or it will break you—daily.

But these roles are your greatest leadership opportunity and they have the power to shape you into the man and leader God created you to be. Engage in life-changing discussions with other men to grow in your character as a man in community with others!

$10.99 paperback

112 pages

ISBN: 978-1-946453-81-5

https://beresolute.org/product/20-lessons-that-build-a-mans-family/

THE MEN'S DAILY DEVO:
Short, Sweet, and To The Point

Do you need a great daily devotional made just for men? If you have not tapped into the Men's Daily Devotional, then you need to get it today. It consists of short, daily devotionals that you can use and share with other men. You can subscribe on the website.

www.beresolute.org/mdd

CPSIA information can be obtained
at www.ICGtesting.com
Printed in the USA
LVHW090409110222
710655LV00005B/586